D1388012

BIBLE KEY WORDS

III. SIN

MANUALS FROM KITTEL

Translated and edited by

J. R. COATES

———

FIRST TITLES

I. LOVE

II. THE CHURCH

III. SIN

IV. RIGHTEOUSNESS

BIBLE KEY WORDS
FROM GERHARD KITTEL'S
*THEOLOGISCHES WÖRTERBUCH
ZUM NEUEN TESTAMENT*

SIN

BY

GOTTFRIED QUELL
GEORG BERTRAM
GUSTAV STÄHLIN AND
WALTER GRUNDMANN

LONDON
ADAM AND CHARLES BLACK
SOHO SQUARE

THIS EDITION FIRST PUBLISHED 1951
BY A. AND C. BLACK LIMITED
4, 5 AND 6 SOHO SQUARE LONDON W.1

Translated from the German
first edition, Stuttgart, 1933
with additions by Walter
Grundmann and J. R. Coates

MADE IN GREAT BRITAIN
PRINTED AT THE UNIVERSITY PRESS
ABERDEEN

PREFACE

" THE whole nature of the Christian religion stands upon these two great pillars, namely, the greatness of our fall and the greatness of our redemption." These words of William Law are echoed by modern theologians. William Temple, e.g., says in his Gifford Lectures (1934), " The centre of trouble is the personality as a whole, which is self-centred and can only be wholesome and healthy if it is God-centred. . . . Man cannot meet his own deepest need, nor find for himself release from his profoundest trouble. What he needs is not progress, but redemption." * Leonard Hodgson, critical of Temple, says " Sin, then, is the heart of the problem ; what account are we to give of it ? In one sense, no account can be given of it beyond saying that it is the choice of what is wrong because of some desirable quality in it. It is an irrational act, and is therefore incapable of explanation, a surd in the order of reality, opaque to thought, unintelligible. All attempts to give an intelligible account of it explain it away and describe it as something other than what it really is, as is invariably done by philosophers of the school of absolute idealism. . . . A revelation of enlightenment might be adequate to a universe in which evil was at bottom an unreality which could be thought away ; but in this universe in which evil is the grim reality we know it to be, the divine Word must be an act of redemptive power. The heart of the Christian gospel is the proclamation of this act of redemption as a fact of history, or rather, as the central fact of all history." †

* *Nature, Man and God*, pp. 367 and 513.
† *Towards a Christian Philosophy*, pp. 184 and 186.

v

This is an age of anodynes. Feelings are blunted by much sophistication ; and an urgent problem is how to resensitise modern man. What will break up the cynical determinism that prevails so widely ? Some may think that the panic fear of war will banish man's fear of facing the spectre within, so that the long repression may be ended, and the truth bring freedom. But what will unveil the truth ?

The Greeks and the psychologists can bring us to a deep level of analysis, when we try to be honest with ourselves—when we cease from our multitudinous escapist activities and look inwards—but they do not bring us to the bottom of things. Only the Word of God can do that, penetrating the last screens of self-deceit and making us ashamed of ourselves ; and the Word is spoken in the Bible. The present volume helps us to understand that Word.

Gottfried Quell's exposition of the story of the Fall is a notable contribution to Bible study, and will help the preacher as well as the theologian—and the sinner. Georg Bertram's examination of the theology of the Septuagint is a valuable piece of pioneer work, and may well stimulate others to study what Swete called the " dogmatic interest " of the Greek translators. Gustav Stählin laid the foundation for the rest of the article before he went to India, and the work was completed by Walter Grundmann, of Jena, with contributions from Hermann Kleinknecht and Karl Georg Kuhn. The section dealing with ἁμαρτωλός and ἀναμάρτητος was made into a separate article by Karl Heinrich Rengstorf, and we much regret that we are not able to include it in the present volume.

When the article was published in 1933, Dr. Grundmann was a Pastor in Saxony. During the war he was made prisoner by the Russians, and after his release at the end of 1945 gave himself to social and theological work. Eventually he was appointed to an evangelical Pastorate in Waltershausen, a town of 12,000 inhabitants in the Thüringer Wald. In addition to his work for the Kittel Dictionary, Dr. Grundmann's most important writings are *Die Gotteskindschaft in der Geschichte Jesu und ihre religionsgeschichtlichen Voraussetzungen* (1938) ; "Aufnahme und Deutung der Botschaft Jesu im Urchristentum" (*Gotteskindschaft*, Vol. II, 1941) ; *Jesus der Galiläer und das Judentum* (1941) ; "Die Bergrede Jesu" (*Akad. Antrittsrede*, 1939) ; "Das Problem des hellenistischen Christentums innerhalb der Jerusalemer Urgemeinde (*Z.N.W.* XXXVIII, 45-73, 1939) ; "Die Apostel zwischen Jerusalem und Antiochia" (*Z.N.W.* XXXIX, 110-137, 1940). We are grateful to him for a number of additions to his chapter on "Sin in the New Testament", specially written for this translation, viz. pp. 66, line 12— 68, 9 ; 67, notes ; 69, 3-70, 8 ; 70, 19-26 ; 76, 17-77, 7 ; 77, note 1 ; 81, 8-21 ; 83, 6-16 and note 1 ; 84, 6-12 ; 85, 35-86, 10.

Work on the Dictionary goes ahead under Gerhard Friedrich, of Bethel, the 5th Volume being well under way. Volumes I-IV (A-N) are being reprinted, and I-III are now available (price 48, 60 and 69 marks respectively). The publisher, W. Kohlhammer, of Stuttgart, is to be congratulated on the great success of a great enterprise.

J. R. COATES.

CONTENTS

BIBLIOGRAPHY

CHAPTER I

K. UMBREIT : Die Sünde, ein Beitrag z. Theol. d. A.T., 1853.

J. C. MATHES : Theologisch Tijdschrift XXIV, 225 ff., 1890.

J. KÖBERLE : Sünde u. Gnade im relig. Leben d. Volkes Israel, 1905.

W. STAERK : Sünde u. Gnade nach d. Vorstellung d. älteren Judentums, 1905.

F. BENNEWITZ : Die Sünde im alten Israel, 1907.

H. SEEGER : Die Triebkräfte d. rel. Lebens in Israel u. Babylon, 1923.

S. MOWINCKEL : Psalmenstudien I, 39 ff., 1921.

J. PEDERSEN : Israel, its Life and Culture, 411 ff., 1926.

J. HEMPEL : Zeitschr. f. syst. Theol. X, 163-199, 1932.

CHAPTER II

[C. H. DODD : The Bible and the Greeks, 76-81, 1935.]

CHAPTER III

F. WEBER : Jüdische Theologie, 2nd edn., 1897.

F. C. PORTER : The Yeçer Hara' (Yale), 1902.

W. BOUSSET—H. GRESSMANN : Die Rel. d. Jud., 3rd ed., 399-409, 1926.

G. F. MOORE : Judaism, 1927 ff.

A. BÜCHLER : Studies in Sin, etc. in Rabb. Lit. of 1st century, 1928.

CHAPTERS IV—VI

H. CREMER—J. KÖGEL : Bibl.-theol. Wörterb. d. N.T. Gr., 11th ed., 1923.

R. C. TRENCH : Synonyms of the N.T., 8th ed., 1876.

E. D. BURTON : Galatians (I.C.C.), 436 ff., 1921.

H. LIETZMANN : Römer, 3rd ed., 75 ff., 1928.

M. DIBELIUS : Die Geisterwelt im Gl. d. Paulus, 119 ff., 1909.

R. OTTO : Sünde und Urschuld, 1932.
    (See also works on N.T. Theology.)

Chapter V

K. Latte : Schuld u. Sünde in der greich. Rel. (A.R.W., XX, 254-298, 1920-21).

L. Hey : Ἀμαρτία (Philologus LXXXIII, 1-17, 137-163, 1927).

J. Stenzel : Metaphysik d. Altertums (Hdbch. d. Philosophie, 17 ff., 1929-31).

H. Weinstock : Sophokles, 1931.

F. X. Steinleitner : Die Beicht, etc. in d. Antike (München Diss., 1913).

General

[G. Aulen : Christus Victor (Eng. Trans.), 1931.

E. Brunner : Man in Revolt, esp. VI and VII.

J. Müller : The Christian doctrine of Sin (Eng. Trans.), 1876.

R. Niebuhr : The Nature and Destiny of Man, I, vii-x.

W. E. Orchard : Modern Theories of Sin, 1909.

H. W. Robinson : Recent Reconstruction of the Concept of Sin (E.T.), 1925-26.

C. Schweitzer (Editor) : Krankheit und Sünde.

F. R. Tennant : The Concept of Sin.
The Origin and Propagation of Sin.
Sources of the doctr. of the Fall and Original Sin.

N. P. Williams : The ideas of the Fall and of Original Sin, 1927.]

Note.—Square brackets indicate additions by the translator.

ABBREVIATIONS

A.R.W.	Archiv f. Religionswissenschaft.
C.B.	Cambridge Bible for Schools and Colleges.
Ditt. Syll.	W. Dittenberger, Sylloge Inscript. Graec.
E.T.	Expository Times.
G.V.I.	R. Kittel, Geschichte d. Volkes Israel.
I.C.C.	International Critical Commentary.
LXX.	Septuagint.
R.G.G.	Religion in Geschichte u. Gegenwart, 2nd ed.
Str-Bill.	Strack-Billerbeck, Komm. z. N.T. aus Talmud u. Midrasch.
Winer.	G. B. Winer, Gramm. d. n.t. Spr., 2nd ed. by P. Schmiedel.
Z.A.W.	Zeitschrift f. A.T. Wissenschaft.
Z.N.W.	Zeitschrift f. N.T. Wissenschaft.
Z.S.T.	Zeitschrift f. systematische Theologie.

I. SIN IN THE OLD TESTAMENT

1. LINGUISTIC

(a) The idea of sin is expressed in the Old Testament by a great variety of terms, whose differing shades of meaning are not adequately conveyed, either by our word, "sin", or by the Septuagint ἁμαρτία, ἀδικία, ἀνομία, ἀσέβεια, κακία and their derivatives. One of the most striking and instructive illustrations of this may be seen in the fact that we generally use the word, "guilt", as the translation of the Hebrew *'asham, 'awon*, etc., whereas in the Greek Bible the latter is almost always represented by one of the words just mentioned,[1] and the former either by one of them or by some other inappropriate expression.[2] The following statistics show the most important facts concerning LXX usage, and also display the wealth of the Hebrew vocabulary.

ἁμαρτία predominantly for *hatta'th* (238 times) and *'awon* (70). It also represents the derivatives, *het'* (28), *h^ata'ah* (8), *hatta'ah* (1), *hattayah* (1), *hattaya'* (1), and the Inf. *h^ato'* (1). Other Hebrew equivalents are *pesha'* (19), the verb *pasha'* (2), *'asham* (4), *'ashmah* (2), *'ashem* (1), *resha'* (2),

---

[1] Only at Gen. iv, 13, by αἰτία, the most suitable term.
[2] Mostly πλημμέλεια, -λεῖν, "mistake in music" [metaph. in Plato, etc., for "offence"] (22 times); also ἄγνοια (5), βάσανος (4), ἱλασμός (Amos viii, 14 *'ashmath*), καθαρισμός (Prov. xiv, 9). Ἁμαρτία only Lev. v, 7; Numb. xviii, 9 (Plur.); II Kings xii, 16 (Heb. 17); Is. liii, 10; ἀδικία Jer. li (LXX xxviii), 5.

to'ebhah (2), and the clearly theological *ḥºli* (Is.
liii, 4), *maḥshabhah* (Is. lxv, 2), *mºshubhah* (Jer.
xiv, 7), *'ªlilah* (Ezek. xxxvi, 19), Aramaic *'illah*
(Dan. vi, 5), *ra'ah* (Prov. xxvi, 26), *ṭum'ah* (Lev.
xiv, 19), *derekh* (I Kings xxii, 53), Aram. *ḥªbhulah*
(Dan. vi, 23), and *rasha'* in the Hiph'il [but LXX
translator probably read *bºrish'e*] (Dan. xi, 32).

ἀμάρτημα most frequently for *ḥaṭṭa'th*, four
times each for *'awon* and *pesha'*, once each for
ḥeṭ', *resha'*, *derekh* (Hos. x, 13) and *qeçeph* (Numb.
i, 53 by mistake).

ἀμαρτωλός 72 times for *rasha'* and twice for
resha' ; 11 times for *ḥaṭṭa'*, once each for *ḥaṭṭa'ah*
and *hoṭe'*, and twice for the verb *ḥaṭa'* ; once each
for *ḥaneph*, *ra'*, *ḥoresh* (Ps. cxxviii (cxxix), 3,
theological).

ἀμαρτάνω 162 times for *ḥaṭa'* Qal and twice for
the Hiph'il ; also for the verbs *pasha'* (Lam.
iii, 42), *'asham* (3 times), *ma'al*, *shaḥath* Pi'el
(once), *'asah* (e.g. Numb. v, 7) and *rasha'* Hiph.
(each 3 times) ; and, by mistake or as intentionally free translation, for the nouns *ḥaṭṭa'th* (e.g.
Gen. iv, 7 ; I Sam. xx, 1), *ḥaṭṭa'*, *ḥeṭ'*, and *pesha'*
(each 3 times), *'ashem*, *'ashmah*, *rasha'* (each twice),
and once for *'awon*.

ἀδικία : of the 36 Hebrew equivalents, the
commonest is *'awon* (50 times), whereas *pesha'*
only occurs 7 times, *ḥaṭṭa'th* (Dan. ix, 24) and
'asham (Jer. li (xxviii), 5) each once. Others are
'awlah (14), *'awal* (9), *'awen* (8), *ḥamaṣ* (8), *sheqer*
(7, only in Ps.), *ra'ah* (4), *'osheq* (4), Though
only found once or twice each, the following are
also relevant : *resha'*, *ma'al*, *ḥawwah*, *'awwah*
(Ezek. xxi, 32), *'awwal*, Aram. *'ªwaya'* (Dan. iv,
24), *ra'*, *muṭṭeh*, *mirmah*, *ma'aseh*, *'eseq* (Gen.
xxvi, 20), *meri* (Ezek. xii, 2).

ἀδίκημα 5 times for ʿawon, 4 for peshaʿ, twice for ʿosheq, once each for ḥamaṣ, ʿawlah, raʿ, raʿah, mishpaṭ.

ἄδικος 33 times for sheqer (as nomen rectum [or Genitive]), 10 times for ḥamaṣ, 8 times for ʿawlah. It also represents ʿawel (4), rashaʿ (4), ʿawwal (3), ʿawen, mirmah, ʿosheq, raʿ each twice, and tahpukhah, nᵉbhalah, rᵉmiyyah, tohu each once.

ἀδικέω 3 times for ḥṭʾ, once each for pshʿ, rʿʿ, rshʿ Hiphʿil. On the other hand, 14 times for ʿshq, and 3 times for mʿl (Dan. ix, 5 Theod. (A) for mrd). The relevant nouns are ḥamaṣ (2) and mᵉshubhah (1).

ἀνομία represents 24 Hebrew words : ʿawon (63), ʾawen (26), toʿebhah (26, all in Ezek. except 1 at Jer. xvi, 18), peshaʿ (20, and also the verb at Is. liii, 12), rishʿah (8), reshaʿ (5), zimmah, ḥamaṣ, ʿawlah, ḥaṭṭaʾth (each 7) ; less frequently bᵉliyyaʿal, beçaʿ, derekh, hawwah, maʿal, maʿᵃlal, ʿᵃlilah, nᵉbhalah, mispaḥ (Is. v, 7), ṣarah, ʿawel, ʿoçebh (Ps. cxxxix, 24, perhaps for dᵉbhar-ʿeçebh, as Gunkel suggests), ʿathaq, qalon, sheqer, and once the verb shḥth Hiphʿil.

ἄνομος 31 times for rashaʿ, but only once for ḥaṭṭaʾ (Is. xxxiii, 14) ; elsewhere for ʾawen (5), ḥaneph, ʿawwal, holel, ʿawon (2), etc.

ἀνόμημα is less frequent, standing for ʿawon (3), peshaʿ (3), zimmah (2), ḥaṭṭaʾth (2), and nᵉbhalah, toʿebhah, tiphlah once each.

ἀνομεῖν for rshʿ (Qal and Hiphʿil 8 times), pshʿ (3), shḥth (Piʿel and Hiph. 3) ; also for ʿwh, mʿl, ḥṭʾ (Theod. Dan. ix, 5 ?) and some nouns.

ἀσέβεια next to ἁμαρτία the most definitely religious term, generally represents peshaʿ (27 times), but also reshaʿ and rishʿah (4), and less frequently hawwah, zadhon, zimmah, ḥamaṣ, mirmah, ṣarah, *ᵃlilah, raʿah, toʿebhah*, etc. There are only two cases each of *ḥaṭṭaʾth* and *ʿawon*, and these are not well attested.

ἀσεβής stands almost exclusively for *rashaʿ* (14). ἀσεβεῖν generally for *pashaʿ*, never for *ḥṭ'*. *marah* (Lam. iii, 42) should be noted.

κακία usually for the derivatives of *raʿaʿ*, but also, in some MSS. for *ʿawon* (I Chron. xxi, 8 ; Jer. xvi, 18 ; xiii, 22 (A) ; *ʾawen* (Is. xxix, 20) ; *ḥaṭṭaʾth* (Jer. xv, 13 A).

κακός. Besides the regular *raʿ*, the following are noteworthy : *ʾawen* (3), *zimmah* (Prov. x, 23), *ʿamal* (Job xvi, 2), *reshaʿ* (Prov. xvi, 12), *ʿawlah* (Job xxii, 23).

κακοῦν (Is. l, 9) is the rendering of *rashaʿ* Hiphʿil, and κακοποιεῖν (II Sam. xxiv, 17 A) of *ʿawah* Hiph.

Equivalents for *maradh* or *marah* in a religious context are ἀθετεῖν and ἀφιστάναι (both also for *pashaʿ*), ἀμελεῖν (Jer. iv, 17), ἐρίζειν (I Kings xii, 14 f.), παραβαίνειν, παροξύνειν (Numb. xx, 24 : *mᵉrithem ʾeth pi*), μὴ εἰσακούειν (Is. i, 20), and above all παραπικραίνειν (Ezek. ii, 3 for *maradh* and 18 times for *marah* ; Ezek. also has παραπικραίνων for *beyth meri* 9 times).

The limitation of the LXX vocabulary here exposed is not due to the translators' method. The reason for it is to be found in a peculiar difficulty in the Hebrew, which obviously has no single word suitable for religious or theological purposes, like our word, " sin ". All the terms employed in this connexion can also be used for secular purposes, so that we have to be on our guard against over-emphasising their religious connotation. Close examination shows, more or less clearly, that they all involve a rational interpretation of religious phenomena. They do not arise spontaneously from experience, but are the coinage of theology and have different associations. Thus the translator has more scope for the exercise of subjectivity than might have been desired. In some cases a religious flavour is introduced where it is lacking in the Hebrew,[1] and in others the use of a secular word spoils the religious meaning.[2] It is abundantly clear, from the rich variety of terms used, that the Old Testament offers no neat uniform doctrine of sin ; qualifications are always necessary, and all sorts of subsidiary questions are involved in the general problem of sin.

(b) Our word, " sin ", represents four different Hebrew roots, each with its own nuance, which it is difficult for us to reproduce.

ḥṭ'. The verb occurs 177 times in the Qal, including infinitive and participial forms, 32 times in the Hiph'il and 9 in the Hithpa'el. In addition 15 Pi'el forms are found, all denominative, in the privative sense of putting sin away.[3] Some of the Hithpa'el forms accordingly mean absolving oneself. Most of these 223 forms are used in a religious sense.[4]

The commonest noun formed from this root is *ḥaṭṭa'th* (masculine only at Gen. iv, 7—see p. 15, n. 3), which occurs 289 times and is preferred to words coming from other roots. In a large number of cases [5] the meaning corresponds to the privative use of the verb so that it denotes the means of putting away sin or its consequences, and indicates a

---

[1] Cf. e.g. Prov. i, 31, ἀσέβεια for *mo'eçah*, etc.

[2] Cf. e.g. Job ix, 22, δυνάστης for *rasha'*, etc.

[3] Cf. Bauer-Leander, Hist. Gram. d. hebr. Spr. I (1922), 291 ; G. Bergstrasser, Hebr. Gram. II (1929), 94 ; [S. R. Driver, Exod. (C.B. 1911), 324].

[4] For exceptions, see p. 7.

[5] B. Baentsch (on Exod. xxix, 14) enumerates 101 cases.

particular kind of sacrifice, described in Leviticus iv,
1–v, 13.[1] Otherwise it simply means sin, though in
certain cases it may be rendered by a legal term such
as crime or negligence. All the extended forms of the
word, in the plural or with suffixes, could equally
well come from *ḥaṭṭa'ah*, but this only appears twice
(Exod. xxxiv, 7 and Is. v, 18). *ḥᵃṭa'ah* occurs 8
times,[2] and the masculine *ḥeṭ'* 35 times.[3] *ḥaṭṭa'* (sinner)
occurs 18 times in the plural, but only in the singular
at Amos ix, 8, where it is feminine.

psh' (rebel) as verb 41 times, including Qal parti-
ciple (10) ; as noun 92 times (sing. and plur.).

'wh occurs in 17 verbal forms, of which, however,
perhaps 6 (Niph. and Pi.) have the secular meaning,
" twist ", either literally or metaphorically (see p. 20).
The noun *'awon*[4] has a much stronger religious tone,
stressing the idea of guilt. It occurs 227 times.[5]

shghh (err) as verb 19 times, with the parallel

---

[1] This meaning, as in the case of *'asham*, is perhaps to be
accounted for by the fact that these were key-words in the
sacerdotal theology, and therefore suitable as headings for groups
of sacrifices. The earliest evidence seems to be that of Ezekiel
(cf. R. Smend [and G. A. Cooke] on Ezek. xl, 39). Baentsch
(Lev. 321) assumes a connexion with the pre-exilic fines
(II Kings xii, 16 ; cf. Amos ii, 8) ; but these are only analogies,
—they do not represent a stage in the development of ritual
ideology.

[2] Ps. xl, 7, where *ḥᵃṭa'ah* seems to mean sin-offering, as *ḥaṭṭa'th*
and *ḥaṭṭa'ah* do elsewhere, must have been pointed by someone
with a phrase like *'awen wa 'ᵃçarah* (Is. i, 13) in mind.

[3] *ḥeṭ'* often indicates guilt : Lev. xix, 17 ; xx, 20 ; xxii, 9 ;
xxiv, 15 ; Numb. ix, 13 ; xviii, 22 ; Is. liii, 12 ; Ezek. xxiii, 49.
(See pp. 21 ff.)

[4] Formed from the root, which ends in a vowel, by the addition of the suffix -*an*. Cf. J. Barth, Die Nominalbildung in
d. sem. Spr., 1889, 326.

[5] Other derivatives from the same root, such as *'iy*, *'iw'im*
and *mᵉ'i*, are far removed from the language of religion, with
the possible exception of *'iw'im* in Is. xix, 14.

shghgh (4) and the noun *sheghaghah* (19), expresses the idea of sin as creaturely going astray.[1]

These four roots, though closely related to one another in their religious and theological use, differ from one another so fundamentally in their essential quality that a study of them will enable us to trace the main lines of Hebrew thought on the subject of sin. (Of the words listed above under (*a*), *mrdh* and *mrh* go with *psh'*; *rsh'*, *'wl*, *'shm* should also be considered.)

2. LEGAL AND THEOLOGICAL

(*a*) The statistics show that *ht'* and its derivatives play the principal part in expressing the idea of sin, no doubt because this root conveyed a clear objective picture to the mind, with no reference to motive or to the inner quality of sinful behaviour. Its pictorial character must have been obvious to all who used it. There are a few places in the Old Testament where the word means literally missing the mark, and this must be the clue to its religious, legal and ethical significance. Thus Prov. xix, 2 : " misseth his way " (R.V.m.) ; Prov. viii, 36 : " misseth me " (R.V.m.) contrasted with " findeth me " in ver. 35 ; Job v, 24 : " shalt miss nothing " (R.V.), i.e. " shalt find what thou seekest " ; Judg. xx, 16 : " every one could sling stones at an hair breadth, and not miss ".[2] Ps. xxv, 8 provides an instructive example : the author obviously wrote *hote'im* [Moffatt, " going astray "], meaning those who, with the best will in the world, yet miss the mark (LXX ἁμαρτάνοντας ἐν ὁδῷ), but the Massoretic editors pointed this as *hatta'im* (sinners), in order to convey the idea that

[1] Also *sheghey'ah* (Ps. xix, 13), *mishgeh* (Gen. xliii, 12) and *meshughah* (Job xix, 4).   [2] LXX οὐκ ἐξαμαρτάνοντες.

even those who look to Yahwe for guidance feel
themselves to be sinners. What made it possible to
read this fine idea into the text was the fact that the
author had already used the word metaphorically.
It follows from these examples, even though they are
not very numerous,[1] that *ḥṭ'* never quite lost the sense
of making a mistake ; the commonest expression for
sin in Hebrew lacks the deep religious quality of our
word.

This conclusion is supported by many passages in
the O.T., in which *ḥṭ'* expresses a legal idea, either in
the wording of a law or in the context. Originally
denoting a faulty action, it came to be applied to
all kinds of wrong-doing. This can be seen wherever
it indicates failure to comply with the normal laws of
human intercourse. In the law concerning witnesses,
Deut. xix, 15-21, *ḥaṭṭa'th*, like *'awon*, means any
breach of the civil law : there is no reference to religion or the cult ; the case is tried in a secular court.[2]
Similarly, at Deut. xxi, 22, *ḥeṭ'* means an ordinary
criminal case (*mishpaṭ*).[3] There is a special reference
to legal proceedings in the threat (Is. xxix, 21) against

---

[1] In Is. lxv, 20, *ḥaḥoṭe'* means " he that falls short " of a full
life,—a parallel to " an old man that hath not filled his days ".
He is only a sinner from the point of view of the dogma that
untimely death is evidence of sin.

[2] Most modern commentators regard the verse as awkwardly
expanded by the introduction of Yahwe and the priests. [" But
it is quite as probable that *before the LORD* was all that the
original text of the law contained " (G. A. Smith *ad loc.*, C.B.
1918).]

[3] Like Deut. xxii, 26. [G. A. Smith : " This compound
phrase seems a fusion of *a sin of death*, a capital sin, xxii, 26, and
a sentence of death, a capital charge, xix, 6. Or *mishpaṭ* is a gloss."]
On the other hand a religious tone is given to *ḥeṭ'* by the mention
of an appeal to Yahwe at Deut. xv, 9 ; xxiii, 22 ; xxiv, 15.
As the protector of right, he is affected by any departure from
the norm.

those who compel people to make false statements : *mah^aṭi'e 'adham b^edhabhar* ; and Hezekiah is obviously using legal terminology when he says *haṭa'thi* to the king of Assyria (II Kings xviii, 14).[1] It is with the same word that Jephthah meets the Moabite king : " I have done no wrong to you " [Moffatt] ; the reference is to the common practice in international relations (Judg. xi, 27). Breaches of the civil law are indicated on the part of Joseph's fellow-prisoners by the employment of the verb at Gen. xl, 1 (E? J?) and the noun at xli, 9.[2] The verb also occurs in the account of David's loyalty to Saul, and the latter's disloyalty (I Sam. xix, 4 ; xxiv, 12 ; xxvi, 21), referring to the ordinary laws of personal relationship.

Other examples border very closely on the forensic, even though they speak of deviation from an ethical, rather than a legal norm. When Reuben (Gen. xlii, 22 E)[3] and Jonathan (I Sam. xix, 5) use the word, they are speaking of murder. On the lips of Jacob (Gen. xxxi, 36) and Abimelech (Gen. xx, 9) it means things that " are not done ". It can even denote a continuing state of guilt or moral boycott, as in the case of Judah (Gen. xliii, 9 J ; cf. xliv, 32), who is obviously describing the unfortunate consequences for himself if he fails to fulfil his promise.

(*b*) Our brief study of the usage of *ht'* [4] lays the

---

[1] Exod. v, 16 (pointing *w^eḥaṭṭa'th 'immakh* with Symmachus) voices an appeal against unjust treatment.

[2] Obviously there can be no reference on the part of the Hebrew writer to the divinity of the Pharaoh.

[3] Cf. the self-accusation of the brothers in ver. 21 : *'^ashemim '^anaḥnu.*

[4] A similar picture is presented by *rasha'*, which is more definitely legal in character. In law it means the one who is in the wrong : e.g. Exod. xxiii, 1. That gives rise to all its other shades of meaning. Cf. G. Marschall, Die " Gottlosen " des erstens Psalmenbuches, 1929, 49 ff.

foundation for an understanding of its religious
significance, and indeed of the O.T. doctrine of sin
as a whole. In the case of the other roots mentioned
above, we cannot trace with the same historical
accuracy the development from colloquial and legal
to theological and religious usage ; whereas this one
clearly involves the presupposition that the religious
life is subject, or ought to be subject, to legal norms or
at least to generally recognised rules. If the religious
life is regarded predominantly as being under rules
and regulations, intercourse with God being possible
only under prescribed conditions, then we have here
a specifically theological consideration. It would be
possible, if it were so desired, to regard theology as
the clue to the whole process of the transference of
meaning, and this could not be disproved by the
quotation of any passage in the O.T. But we cannot
help feeling a certain fundamental hesitation about
making theology responsible for the coining of ideas
so deeply rooted in the flesh and blood of those who
express them, especially in view of the fact that roots
like *psh'* are not merely, like *ht'* and *'wh*, formal in
character, but also include the idea of human motive.

psh' represents sin under its most active, and therefore least formal aspect. E. König suitably equates
it with practising rebellion (Rebellion üben).[1] In
secular, non-legal speech it means the wilful breaking
of a relationship of loyalty and peace, as when Israel
broke away from the house of David (I Kings xii, 19),
or Edom from the " hand " of Judah (II Kings viii, 20).
When Isaiah (i, 2) depicts the opposition of Israel
to Yahwe as the rebellion of sons against their father,
or Jeremiah (ii, 29) draws a parallel between their
rebellion and the initiation of legal proceedings against
Yahwe, human responsibility for the situation, i.e.

[1] E. König, Wörterbuch, s.v.

for sin, is unmistakable.[1] Amos has no need to explain his cry, " transgress " : that one word, *pish^eu*
(iv, 4) is all that is required to indicate Israel's almost
instinctive self-assertion and defiance of God. Expressions like these imply a numinous element underlying sin ; rebellion is a consciously willed " offence
not against a mere whim, but against a numinous
object of worth—whatever it may be ".[2] Sin is then
a spontaneous human reaction to the holy and the
godlike.

The same thought is involved in the idea of " erring
and straying " in our relations with God, which brings
out the tragic element in human experience. Though
often unobserved, the essentially theological problem
of sin comes into view here, compelling our attention.
Unfortunately *shaghah* (err) appears in the O.T.
mostly in a rather feeble way in the terminology of
ritual, as though it had lost its original force ; or
perhaps we should put the matter the other way
round, and say that at first its true value was developed by a few religious thinkers from its relatively
harmless connexion with ritual. It is this connexion
which has made it appear to be the weakest of the
words for sin, indicating as it does, not culpable
negligence but ignorance (Ezek. xlv, 20 ; Lev. iv, 2, 13,
etc.). Similarly, in the law concerning cities of refuge,
the noun *sh^eghaghah* is used for " unintentional "
manslaughter (Numb. xxxv, 11 ; Josh. xx, 3). In

---

[1] For further examples see Hos. vii, 13 ; viii, 1 (rebellion
against Yahwe's Torah) ; Jer. ii, 29 ; iii, 13 ; Ezek. xviii, 31 ;
xx, 38 ; Is. xliii, 27 (parallel to *het'*). Ps. v, 10 (Heb. 11) shows
how closely *pesha'* and *marah* are related to each other, and how
both bring out the part played by the will. The enemies' plans,
which prove to be their downfall, are parallel to their acts of
rebellion, and both are summed up in the final *maru bhakh*,
" they bid thee defiance ".

[2] Cf. R. Otto, Sünde und Urschuld, 1932, 4.

all these cases the hidden force of the word is lost. *Shaghah* is by no means a mild expression. It is really much more weighty than the terms which indicate a formal missing of the mark or an emotional rebellion, since it implies a right intention on the part of the one who goes astray ; his going wrong is to be attributed to circumstances, i.e. from the religious point of view, to God. An element of demonic horror comes upon the scene the moment error is viewed religiously apart from ritual, and indeed is not entirely absent from the latter, in spite of the possibility of accommodation, so far as the cult is concerned. Job's remark, that he who is misled and he who misleads both belong to God, is not just a harmless truism (Job xii, 16) : he is voicing the alarm and agony of the thought that man, struggling towards God, cannot reach the goal because God denies him the ability to do so. The bitter poet, relentlessly analysing his own spiritual life, lays resolutely upon God the responsibility for man's fatal incapacity. Job holds himself justified in disputing the matter with God.

Isaiah's mind seems to have moved in the same direction, though he never reached such a titanic outburst of despair. He launches out (xxviii, 7 f.) against those whose business it is to lay down the law about going astray, on the ground that they themselves have gone astray in drunken folly. His painful realism brings out the double meaning of *shaghah*—reeling under the influence of drink and getting off the track in religion—thus laying the blame for their behaviour half upon themselves and half upon God, whose messengers they are. What he thinks of, when he uses the word, is the contemplation of God with minds beclouded and incompetent. God will speak to those who " err ", with " stammering lips and another tongue " which they cannot under-

stand. They will know the suffering of Job, who
finds no escape from his error, in spite of every human
effort to comfort him, but must endure the torture of
the mystery of God (Job xix, 4 ; vi, 24). Doubtless
many failed to perceive, or were unwilling to perceive, the dread import of this word, *shaghah*. It is
certainly missed by the quiet man of simple faith to
whom we owe Psalm cxix, as it was by Job's friends :
all he knows is that formerly he went astray, but the
Law has been his teacher and he has learned a lesson
from his affliction (Ps. cxix, 67).

Although recognition of the irrational factor in sin
is not lacking in Hebrew, as may be seen in *pasha'*,
marah, and *shaghah*, it must be admitted that, apart
from *pasha'*, it does not play a predominant part. It
seems to have been largely displaced in the O.T. by
the idea of ceremonial impurity. This is a less primitive conception, being fundamentally theological in
character, owing to its connexion with a more or less
established doctrine of God. It is, of course, hardly
possible apart from explicitly theological texts like
the codes of law in the Pentateuch, to say how far
O.T. writers had theological considerations in mind
—or whether they had any at all. Logical structure
is usually in inverse ratio to lively feeling. Yet even
in such cases one can recognise the underlying idea
of missing the mark or offending against the norm,
and it is easy to reconstruct the relevant doctrine.
We must certainly beware against what Gunkel
called " over-heightening " in the exegesis of O.T.
passages dealing with sin. But the O.T. itself obviously feels the need of further definition from time
to time, when it adds a phrase like " with a high
hand " (Numb. xv, 30). The so-called " sin " of
Sodom and Gomorrah (Gen. xviii, 20) was not sin
in the eyes of the inhabitants of those cities : it was

first recognised as such by the Israelite narrator on the ground of a theological judgment. Many other statements about sin are more naturally associated with the authors' theories than with numinous feelings. This has to be remembered even in the interpretation of prayers in which sins are confessed. Thus, e.g., in Ps. xxxii suffering leads to reflexion, and this again to the confession of sin. One cannot help suspecting that many an action comes in this way to be branded as sin, which was never directed against God, and that God is regarded as keeping a sharp watch over the performance of ceremonies and the technique of ritual.

(c) Scepticism as to the specifically religious character of the prevailing idea of sin in the O.T. is strengthened by the fact that the Wisdom movement in Israel fostered an emphatically intellectual conception of it. There were no doubt good pedagogical reasons for this, but one cannot resist the impression that such doctrine was popular, and that it was the sort of thing that Isaiah was making fun of, with his " precept upon precept, line upon line " (Is. xxviii, 10). A fool (nabhal),[1] according to the wise men, is a man who does not know his duty towards God, or, if he does know it, fails to realise that his success in life depends upon his performing that duty (Ps. xiv, 2 etc.). The pious man's feeling of superiority as thus expressed, is always objectionable, even though the same kind of argument is occasion-

[1] Cf. also $k^e ṣil$, Prov. iii, 35, etc. ; he is stupid like the beasts (ba'ar) Ps. xcii, 6 (Heb.7), cf. xlix, 10 (11) ; nabhubh, Job xi, 12. It is significant that the simpleton (pethi) can become religiously sensible if he comes under the influence of the Law : Ps. xix, 8 (7) ; cxix, 130. When on the other hand, as is more often the case, such persons are described by words like " cunning ", that is either to be understood as the language of controversy or regarded as an example of primitive thinking.

ally used by Jeremiah (Jer. iv, 22 ; v, 21) and
finds a place in Moses' exhortation (Deut. xxxii, 6).
There may be a touch of pastoral sympathy with the
" foolish people " in such utterances, but they completely fail to give proper expression to the idea of
motive, which is the real characteristic of sin.

Sin's true nature is much more clearly recognised
when the enlarged Decalogue (Exod. xx, 5 ; Deut.
v, 9) designates offenders against the instructions of
Yahwe as " those that hate me ". Nothing could
make it clearer that there is something finally in-
explicable in sin, for the dynamic of hatred lies
beyond human understanding. *R^esha'im* (wicked)[1]
and *leçim* (scorners) too, seem to be full of hatred
towards God, like many other kinds of godless men,
whose designation is for the most part quite obscure
as to etymology and meaning.[2] It can hardly be
claimed that typical scholastic views of sin are conveyed by terms like *to'ebhah* (abomination), *zimmah*
(device), *'awen* (trouble), *ḥamaṣ* (violence), *r^emiyyah*
and *mirmah* (deceit), *b^eliyya'al*,[3] *hol^elim*, etc.

The words just mentioned lack the peculiar preg-
nancy of terms like *ḥeṭ'*, *pesha'*, *'awon*—that quality
which has given them their place in the language
of piety as simple metaphors, unencumbered with
theological speculation. If this seems to mean that
the complete and unmistakable idea of sin was a
comparatively late growth on Israelite soil, such a

[1] The Book of the Covenant (cf. Exod. xxiii, 7) emphasises
Yahwe's antipathy to the *rasha'*, which may be the reply to his
antipathy to Yahwe (cf. also Exod. ix, 27).

[2] Cf. esp. Mowinckel and Pedersen (see p. xi), and Marschall,
op. cit., esp. 125.

[3] Cf. esp. Ps. xviii, 4 (5), where the reference is to a demon
dwelling in Sheol. Similarly, at Gen. iv, 7, *ḥaṭṭa'th* represents
a demonic being. Cf. H. Duhm, Die bösen Geister im A.T.,
1904, 8 f.

conclusion can hardly invalidate our thesis.[1] It rather attests the full maturity of a form of religious expression, based on immovable categories, the validity of which no-one, at that stage of culture, was in a position to dispute. Nothing could show the simple man more simply and clearly why his heart was restless in the presence of the holy than the use of words which meant missing the mark, rebelling against the normal, or going astray and needing to find the right way again. By the employment of these pregnant terms conduct was judged, responsibility was fixed, and above all the demand of God's will was sternly recognised, so that they came to have the value of formulae, giving forceful expression to man's sense of creaturehood amid the trials of life. If the religion of Israel recognised the will of God as the supreme and universal law, then it must try to bring home to men the fact of their separation from God, and hostility towards him, by means of ideas which had binding force because they indicated the direction in which human life ought to move. Now this is exactly what we find : in *ḥaṭa'* as a verb of motion, or in *'iwwah*, in the thought of going astray, and in the legal implications of *pasha'*—all thoroughly typical of Hebrew idiom. No doubt it took many generations of theological thinking to work all this out, at least theoretically, and it cannot be denied that the whole development was closely bound up with the idea of the Covenant, which forms the basis of Israelite religion.[2] In both cases the feeling of fear is repressed by a sense of responsibility which

[1] The absence of the idea of sin from our earliest specimens of O.T. literature may be accidental, and has no evidential value.

[2] Cf. Dan. xi, 32 : *marshi'e b*e*rith* (who bring guilt upon the covenant), and Pedersen, op. cit., 415 : " The breach of the covenant is the kernel of sin ". [Cf. p. 2.]

increases with a growing apprehension of the greatness of God, and covers the whole of life when it surrenders all to him in the confession (Ps. li, 4) : " Against thee only have I sinned " (literally, " in relation to thee only have I missed the mark ").

This shows clearly how sin differs from other kinds of failure. In order to ascertain what sin really is, we must exclude all human opinion as to the meaning of what has happened. Whether man's judgment be severe or lenient, for the suppliant himself only the thought of God and what he has willed can reveal the true character of his failure. He is accountable to no judge but God himself. That is his " wisdom in the hidden part " (Ps. li, 6). He has broken God's rule : that is what he recognises as his sin. He has done what every sinner does, and his action constitutes sinful behaviour as such. To make that stand out sharply, he rounds off his confession with the almost blasphemously disarming words : " I sinned in order that thou mightest be just and clear ", representing as the sinner's aim what was actually the effect of his sinful action on his apprehension of God. He sees now—and this is the climax—how the objective fact of his sinning appears to serve the purpose of leading him to acknowledge the absoluteness of God's law. It may seem strange that he should put this into the form of a rather unhappy negative piece of flattery (the positive follows in the sixth verse) : " I sinned to the glory of God " ; but his assertion is very important from a theological point of view, for it represents a determined effort to find a place for human failure within the divine order, without giving up its religious characterisation as sin.

Hermann Gunkel [1] can hardly be right in suggesting

[1] H. Gunkel, Psalmen, 1926, 226, following B. Duhm. [Oesterley, The Psalms, 1939, 271, 274, seems to hold both views !]

that David could not say he had sinned against God alone, when he has seduced a woman and arranged the murder of her husband. No, David may have committed a crime against Uriah, but it was only in relation to God that this act of oriental despotism was a sin. Ps. li, 4 gives no clue as to what the Psalmist has actually done, and therefore cannot be used to disprove the statement made in the title. Unless this is ruled out for other reasons, it may well be correct, so far as ver. 4 is concerned, for that deals with the resulting religious situation and not with the act itself. To weaken the close of the daring self-accusation by connecting the second half of ver. 4 with ver. 3 [1] is a vague exegetical device which convinces nobody, since it fails to take the author seriously, and casts unnecessary doubt on a textual tradition which there is no reason to suspect. Those who " rejoice in the spiritual depth " [2] of this Psalmist ought to ask themselves whether he really could have expressed himself in such a confused way as is required by this hypothesis. The theory of an " elliptical mode of expression " [3] is afraid to acknowledge the blasphemy involved in the element of flattery ; but this sort of manipulation of the passage remains objectionable, even though it can point to precedents in ancient Israel or the Jewish Church. If the writer had meant this, he would have expressed himself more clearly. The simplest explanation, and therefore surely the right one, is given by W. Staerk.[4] How Paul understood the words under discussion is shown by Rom. iii, 5a.

(d) The O.T. as a whole teaches that sin denotes

---

[1] Duhm and Gunkel.   [2] Gunkel, 225.

[3] R. Kittel, Psalmen, 1922, 190.

[4] W. Staerk, Schr. d. A.T., 1920, 231. [See also A. F. Kirkpatrick, C.B., Psalms, 1902, 286, 289.]

abnormal behaviour, from the point of view of both
law and theology. Although the words concerned
are mainly used in a theological sense, the fact that
they are also found in other connexions is highly
significant. It should also be observed that the idea,
rationally conceived, belongs much less to religion, the
actual intercourse between God and man, than to
theology, the theoretical elucidation of that intercourse. Such an idea is coined by the latter in an
attempt to define, and so to interpret, a quite distinct
religious situation, or a psychical event. In the
nature of the case, therefore, the O.T. has to use a
large variety of expressions for sin. These are best
interpreted as formulae representing different theological views. They are efforts to exhibit religious
phenomena, whose background lies beyond human
understanding.

The resultant idea of sin, which justifies and necessi-
tates the bringing together of all these terms, is certainly
many-sided, but nevertheless has a real unity. This is
indeed emphasised by the way in which the O.T.
itself brings the words together—as poetical synonyms
(Ps. xxxii, 5), or for impressiveness (Exod. xxxiv, 7),[1]
or sometimes, whether intentionally or not, with the
effect of bringing to the fore certain shades of meaning :
e.g. Job xxxiv, 37 points to a gradation (" he adds
pesha' to his *hatta'th* "), and at Lev. xvi, 21 (cf. ver. 16)
the addition of the word *hatta'th* gives a special character to *'awen* and *pesha'*.[2] It is obvious that all
variations mean fundamentally one and the same
thing, viz., deviation from a prescribed norm, which
is what the predominant root *ht'* means. The number

[1] Here also belong Ezek. xxi, 19, and Dan. ix, 24. On all
these passages see L. Köhler, Z.A.W., 1928, 214.

[2] Hos. xii, 9, is less significant, since the punctuation is out of
order.

of different roots available provides amply for the
presentation of all sorts of views and judgments on
the subject. Sometimes the emphasis is on the
psychical aspect, sometimes on the sinful act itself,
and sometimes on the resultant situation. But usually
it is not the root itself, but the context, which brings
out precisely the thought and feeling behind the
words, and determines their religious significance,
which is not always immediately obvious.

Careful examination of the relevant passages makes
it possible to differentiate a whole series of stages,
from simple objectivity to the unmistakable encounter
with God. Even in the case of a religious utterance
which seems to be almost entirely free from theology,
the idea never completely loses its theoretical colouring,
just because it remains an idea, and, as such, easily
leads to a rational and juristic view of the subject ;
and this, however valuable from an educational point
of view, always tends to rob religious phenomena of
the very variety indicated by the use of different
terms. Those roots especially which connote deviation from a norm (ht', $'wh$, $shghh$, $t'h$, etc.) have a
pictorial quality which is hardly suitable for the
religious situation to which they point. All they can
do is to establish the fact that something is out of
order. On the other hand, a root like psh' (rebel)
gets much nearer to the real problem of the origin
and meaning of sin as a religious phenomenon, because it leaves no doubt as to the sinner's dominant
motive. But actually, even when one of the other
terms is used, the irrational event to which it refers
imparts to it something, more or less, of its own
quality. This is seen, e.g. in prayers, where confession
or lamentation takes the place of theological terminology. The story of the " Fall " is specially instructive, as the only extended treatment in the O.T. of

the religious problem of sin : here are none of the regular technical terms, apart from the quite general idea of evil ; the true nature of sin is shown in quite a different way.

3. SIN AND GUILT

Before analysing the story of the " Fall " and stating its theological import, we must look again at the fact that a considerable number of the Hebrew words for sin frequently seem to justify, or actually demand, the English word " guilt " for their translation. This is always the case when the writer is thinking, not of the sinful action itself, but of the results of an irregularity, the situation created by sin, or the underlying state of mind. It is evident, from their promiscuous use of terms, that the Hebrews attached little importance to the distinction between sin and guilt, the causal connexion being obvious between abnormal behaviour and an abnormal situation.

There is only one root in Hebrew (*'shm*) which expresses quite definitely the ideas of guiltiness and guilt, and its use is almost confined to matters of ritual law,[1] so that its quality is material and objective, meaning uncleanness. Thus " guilt " does not necessarily involve sin in the sense of wilful rebellion against God's ordinance. It is incurred unintentionally, by mistake, and loses much of its force in the sphere of casuistry (see p. 11). At the same time the consequences of such error are regarded almost as seriously as those of other sins. Going wrong by mistake

---

[1] Gen. xxvi, 10, uses it in connexion with the marriage law : guiltiness may be " brought upon " a man by inducing him to commit adultery with the wife of a stranger ; so also at Judg. xxi, 22. The law of property employs terms which are never associated with the religious idea of guilt, e.g. *mashsha'*, *mashsheh*, *n°shi*, *ḥobh*.

(*bish^eghaghah*), i.e. without premeditation—whether through negligence (Lev. iv, 13, 22) or from some other cause (Lev. iv, 2 ; v, 15, 18 ; Numb. xv, 22, etc.) —incurs guilt just as much as premeditated crime, committed " with an high hand " (Numb. xv, 30, cf. the verbs in ver. 31). Even though a man be completely unaware of his error, he still becomes " unclean and guilty " (Lev. v, 2). The ritual for the removal of guilt is the same as that for the restoration of cleanness.[1]

This dynamistic circle of ideas does not provide the background for those statements about guilt which avoid the use of the technical term '*shm*. A favourite expression is '*awon*, the meaning of which is perfectly clear when it is said to be " borne " or " removed " (the verb is *nasa*' in both cases).[2] Ps. xxxii, 1 f. is specially instructive : " Blessed is he whose transgression is forgiven (*n^esuy pesha*'), whose sin is covered (*k^esuy ḥ^aṭa'ah*). Blessed is the man unto whom the LORD imputeth not iniquity ('*awon*)." Here we have the same triad as before (see p. 19), and the emphasis on the element of guilt is unmistakable. The guilt is " an heavy burden " (Ps. xxxviii, 4), which cannot be borne. It is the accumulated guiltiness of a series of sins. It is substantially identical with the suffering that may torment a man, and shows itself through this suffering. When Cain says, " My '*awon* is greater than I can bear " (Gen. iv, 13), the Hebrew word must be understood as meaning two things, as it does in many Psalms of lamentation, viz., misfortune inflicted as punishment, and a state of affairs contradictory to God's standard. Suffering evokes a sense of guilt, or is one with it. The theological and

---

[1] Cf. A. Bertholet, Das Dynamistische im A.T., 1926, 36 f.

[2] This is strangely overlooked by the LXX, which far too often has ἀδικία (80 times), ἁμαρτία (69), or ἀνομία (64) for '*awon*. Cf. p. 5, n. 1.

rational character of the idea of guilt in the O.T. is very clearly brought out by the way in which theories of atonement and retribution, starting from this identification, are worked out from a legal point of view. It was through the application of legal ideas to the relationship between God and sinners, in respect of righteousness divine and human, that the religious conception of guilt was developed from its numinous root. Its full effect upon the thinking of O.T. writers is therefore purposely discussed in connexion with those complexes.

4. THE STORY OF THE FALL (GENESIS III)

(a) The handling of the problem of sin in Gen. iii, in the setting of the Garden of Eden, is notably free from all theories with a legal tendency, and has no bearing on them. The Yahwist author makes fearless and masterly use of primeval mythological material,[1] to show with absolutely convincing simplicity, which a child could understand, how sin happens, what it is, and what it leads to. It is remarkable that in this myth of the so-called " Fall " the usual technical concepts are all lacking, with the exception of the term *ra'*, which is beset with difficulties. The reader is only aware that this is a story about sin.[2]

[1] For the analysis of motives see, in addition to commentaries, H. Gressmann in the Harnack Festgabe, 1921, 24 ff. ; R. Kittel, G.V.I., 1923, 220 f. ; J. Feldmann, Paradies und Sündenfall, 1913. [See J. Skinner, Genesis (1910), 90-97.]

[2] It is hardly correct to say that this view was first taken by the so-called Deuteronomists, as H. Schmidt does in Die Erzählung von Paradies und Sündenfall, 1931, 49 f. The Israelite author knew, as well as all his readers, that sin is the main point of the story. Cf. K. Budde, Die Biblische Urgeschichte, 1883, 72 : " It seems to me that, if the author were to ask the reader what spiritual power the story made him see, the answer could only be, sin." For a discussion of all the problems involved, see now also Budde's Die biblische Paradiesgeschichte, 1932.

The storyteller is giving an object-lesson by means
of a typical scene from life itself, and therefore has to
avoid unsuitable scholastic terms. He leaves theology
to the reader who may be interested in it, merely
hinting at the direction in which he himself thinks it
would be fruitful. His main purpose is to concentrate
attention solely upon what took place, the occurrence
itself which provides the material for theorising. This
is calculated to bring home the fact that our destiny
as men is largely determined by that event. What is
commonly called sin is for this reason presented as
one of a series of happenings, all marked by tension ;
which serves better than theorising to exhibit the
disastrous living reality with which theology, cult and
piety deal so lamely whenever they turn their attention
to sin.

Apart from all conjectures—and a few generally
accepted theories—concerning its provenance, the
story presents the following fundamental ideas.
Yahwe's will for men has been unambiguously expressed in a prohibition, the severity of which is
heightened by the announcement of the dire results
of disregarding it. At first it is not disputed, since
God's authority is beyond dispute. It is only the
clever serpent that is struck by the disproportionate
gravity of the penalty, which is death, in view of the
triviality of the offence. He introduces a discussion
of the subject by asking the woman a question, osten-
sibly about the scope of the prohibition, to which a
negative answer would be expected. Her naïve reply
betrays no trace of scepticism, but opens the door to
it, and gives the serpent the opportunity he wants for
an audacious criticism of the prohibition. He regards
the warning as mere bluff. According to him the
whole business is intended to serve God's own interest
and not that of man, who has to be frightened off

from something which he could easily and safely appropriate by transgressing the prohibition. "Ye shall be as God, knowing good and evil." The woman, already intrigued by the beauty of the forbidden fruit, listens like a fool to the words about being clever, though she hardly understands them—and commits the act of disobedience. The man takes part in the misdeed without a word. He must have heard what the serpent said, since he was with the woman.

The first result of the act of disobedience is that the pair become aware of their nakedness and try to cover it ; the second, that they hide from Yahwe when he draws near ; the third, that the man, when cross-examined, first makes an evasive reply and then tries to explain his conduct ; the fourth, that all concerned fall under Yahwe's condemnation.

It is clear that, in this disastrous chain of consequences, the chief importance belongs to what happens in the spiritual sphere, as suggested by the enigmatic words about being as God and knowing good and evil. Adam and Eve are as God, in that they disregarded his prohibition. This is the immediate result of their being led to doubt, first, whether God's arrangement is in their interest, and, secondly, whether God's will for them is unconditionally binding. We shall not here pursue the point that the story seems to distribute these considerations unequally between the man and the woman. What matters is that it occurs to both of them that they have only to exercise their wills in order to infringe God's regulation. But this can only happen when the self-determining person reaches a positive, binding conviction, such as the serpent has helped to produce by his relentless exposure of obedient faith as mere stupidity. If sin is a breach of God's order, we have here the recognition and characterisation of its driving force. Practical reason, the power to make judgments and act on them, which exalts man to a divine sovereignty in the sphere of his own affairs—that is the germ of sinful behaviour. Reason is able to set aside all correctives, including that of religion, and to launch men upon courses of action which ignore the judgment of God. Nevertheless as a matter of fact, they stand under that judgment.

Beside this picture of bold self-assertion on the part of man, as he becomes conscious of the power of his will, stands the other, which shows how man's assertion of self against God creates a situation in which he dreads the divine scrutiny, how his will, instead of rejecting the call to render an account, collapses miserably, and finally the Godlike one is caught out like a naughty schoolboy, shuffling and sulky.

Adam and Eve are shown up with a rare sarcasm as " knowing good and evil ". This phrase is in apposition to the words about being " as God "— the syntax is no doubt intentionally vague—and means the same thing, though what that is remains entirely uncertain, since both are sarcastic rather than didactic, intended to conceal rather than to reveal. The conjecture that the reference is to puberty seems to rely mainly on the fact that the first result of transgression is the " discovery " [Heb. " knowledge "] of nakedness, and not so much on the fact that " knowledge " is a sexual term [cf. Gen. iv, 1].[1] It is utterly impossible to drag the terms " good " and " evil " into the sexual sphere. It can hardly be suggested that they conveyed that sort of nuance to Hebrew ears ; such a theory is not proved by Prov. xxxi, 12, or Deut. i, 39, and least of all by II Sam. xix, 35 (36). Accordingly, to entitle

---

[1] Gressmann, 46. Cf. E. König, Genesis *ad loc.*

the story, " Origin of physical love ", does not throw much light on the problem.[1] To say " delightful and painful " instead of " good and evil " smacks too much of sentimentality, and does not sound like the Yahwist writer ; it is more like a paraphrase suggested by Clara in Goethe's *Egmont*. When all is said, failing anything better, we may as well accept Wellhausen's robust interpretation of " good and evil " as what we generally call civilisation.[2]

The impression is irresistible that, though the Prometheus motif is unmistakable, it is finally reduced *ad absurdum* by being coupled with the picture of misery. The unsurpassable greatness of the story comes out in the treatment of the ambition to be as God : it is clearly recognised as a grotesque aberration, and yct not held up to contempt and ridicule, but appreciated with the sympathy of one who has himself passed through this humiliating experience. Man's tragic plight, as he struggles in his own strength to overcome his limitations, is so convincingly portrayed in the phrases, " Ye shall be as God " and " To be desired to make one wise ", that it stirs a longing in the breast of every man, from the simplest to the most mature, and presents him with an apology for sin that is alarmingly persuasive. In this way we are brought with the utmost precision to the religious heart of the problem of sin, which is beyond the reach of abstract thought, and consists in man's incontestable inherent right to defy and reject God. A psychological justification of sin is the only way of establishing its reality, and the Yahwist excels all other Biblical writers in the pregnant way in which he achieves this. Man's determination to be civilised, all the work of the creative mind, obeying its

[1] H. Schmidt, op. cit., 22.
[2] Prolegomena 305 ff. (Gesch. Isr. I, 1878, 344 ff.).

own inherent laws, yes, and the impudent insistence of the lusts of the flesh as well, trying to justify themselves theoretically, he grasps them all quite firmly and drags them into the pitiless light of the thought of God. Two worlds confront each other, and the reader can have no doubt that in every act of disobedience to God the same encounter takes place, with its unfathomable distress. Man ventures bravely with varying success, upon the quest of greatness, but in the end he has to seek a hiding-place from the eyes of God ; that is the path laid down for him by the possibilities of his nature. His likeness to God goes to pieces when God calls him.

(b) The story of the " Fall ", as it stands, affords a vista of man's life as a whole. Naturally it is not free from unevennesses and cultural colourings, since it is shot through with mythology. But a theological interpretation, such as that which we are attempting here, must be determined by the unity of the whole complex. As we have it, the tale is aetiological in form, but not obtrusively so, or to the detriment of its convincing force, e.g., in the curses pronounced upon serpent, woman and man, and the peculiar significance attached to nakedness. The common inescapable ills of every-day life are explained as the consequence of our first parents' misbehaviour. Here is the reason why the serpent is such a queer and repulsive creature, why child-bearing is so painful and dangerous, and why man has to sweat for his bread and return to dust at last.[1] But if Adam and Eve share in the common lot, and make themselves clothes like other people, the alleged reason cannot be some-

[1] When A. Menes, in Z.A.W. 1925, 39, suggests that the creation of woman may have been the result of a sin, i.e. an act of divine anger, he is simply indulging his love of hypothesis. J. Hempel seems to me to go too far when he speaks of the suggestion as " fairly certain ", in Zeitschr. syst. Th., 1931, 223.

thing entirely unique, but necessarily implies that what they did is what every human being is capable of doing and must do. Their experience is typical, in its suffering and its shame, and this becomes clearer to the reader the more he begins to understand that their attitude to God is, *mutatis mutandis*, that of every man. For the aetiology of the passage is not merely concerned with the interpretation of pain, labour and death as penalties inflicted by God, or with shame as the consequence of transgression, but also includes, as its most important theme, an interpretation of sin itself as the prime mover and cause of all man's restlessness and misery.[1]

The objections to this aetiological view, expressed by A. Weiser and supported by Gressmann, fail to do justice to the primitive realism of the story.[2]   When we find the ground being cursed for man's sake— an indirect way of speaking of the curse on man himself—we ought not to boggle at the serpent eating dust, which I regard as a townsman's poetic fancy.

The covering of the naked body is also to be understood aetiologically.   It suggests that the feeling of helpless perplexity and uncertainty produced by sin is as typical as the sense of shame evoked by nakedness.   The statement that " they saw that they were naked " is the story-teller's way of establishing the fact that the guilty pair suddenly felt themselves at a loss.   He thinks he can best do this by means of the sense of shame, by raising the question as to its origin and incidentally giving it to be understood that it is a result of sin, something dangerously close to evil, though not identical with it.   Without sin, husband and wife would have had nothing to conceal

[1] This is not the view of M. Weber, Ges. Aufsätze zur Religionssoziologie, 1921, 242.

[2] A. Weiser, Religion u. Sittlichkeit in d. Genesis, 1928, 36 f.

from each other. Their failure has cost them their
simplicity. It is of course true that this line of argument is bound up with a particular cultural view of
nakedness, viz. that of Israel and the Jews, who had
" a holy horror of stripping the body bare ".[1] This,
however, cannot weaken the impression that the
writer definitely intends to draw attention to something which he considers to be of universal validity,
and that in conclusion he actually touches upon a
problem posed by nature and common to all types
of culture, i.e. the sexual question in its broadest
sense.

(c) The aetiological interpretation of the myth of
the " Fall " undoubtedly justifies our basing upon it
a theory of " original sin " in the sense of man's
universal sinfulness.[2] In any case such a theological
deduction would not run counter to the sense of the
myth. Moreover, when the writer attributes the Fall
to man's passionate longing, shown in a thousand
ways, to get knowledge and be clever, he reveals a
very lively apprehension of the fact that all normal
men in every age, not only fall into the same tempta-
tion, but also act in the same way. He knows that if
the intellect is not under control, it fights against
religion, and sin finds a footing in the freedom of will
and thought. As all men have their share of intellect,
with its fatal possibilities, so all are partners in the
incriminating deed, all caught in the web of universal misery.

The story-teller assigns the part of reckless ques-
tioner to the dramatic figure of the serpent, and thus
purposely emphasises the demonic nature of the

---

[1] " Eine ganz und gar rituelle Angst vor der rein physischen
Entblössung " (Weber, op. cit., 205, cf. 234, 245).

[2] Such as is expressed by the same writer at the beginning
and end of his version of the Flood story : Gen. vi, 5 ; viii, 21.

scepticism that bursts all bonds in its fanatical pursuit
of knowledge. He does this in order to stress the
unfathomable dualism that is characteristic of all
sinful behaviour. The sinner, he would say, falls
under a sort of external power, to which he has to
submit, against his better judgment, won over by the
confidence with which it encourages his self-reliance.
The serpent myth is not made to serve any further
purpose in Gen. iii. The writer simply uses its hidden
dualism in order to set forth the analysis of a very
subtle psychical proceeding. The fable is abandoned
as soon as it has made its contribution to the presentation of a comprehensible picture of the woman's
novel procedure. The reader now has a sympathetic
understanding of the way in which physical and
spiritual self-reliance are reinforced by callous doubt,
personified reason's mighty product, and is not sur-
prised when a sudden impulse overrides uncritical
obedience.

No argument from experience can effectively question this account of the way in which one thing leads
to another ; it produces an overwhelming impression
that man's deviation from God's prescribed norm, in
will and deed, is the inevitable outcome of his very
nature ; and this demands the recognition, by every
type of theology, of the universality of the phenomenon
presented in this saga. Undeterred by divine authority, man is determined, and up to a point is able, to
gain knowledge, to discover and anticipate God's
thoughts ; and this leads to a painful tension between
man and God, creating an atmosphere of mistrust, in
which man sees the tempting possibility of abandoning
his proper attitude as a creature, of criticising his
maker, and of thinking and behaving " as God ",
free from control and responsible only to himself.
Born with reason and the ability to pass judgment

upon the world and God, he has the motive for sin, and it is bound to become operative sooner or later, like the rest of his nature.

The more this interpretation is urged from a theological point of view, the more it must be remembered that its starting-point is the realisation that the Yahwist author is not writing a theological treatise, but popularising a fundamental theological idea. He betrays no tendency other than the aetiological, as here set forth. His story, so natural and un-scholastic, is rather the expression of a deep and true piety than of a theology. The relentless pursuit of truth makes it unforgettable. Hardly anywhere else in the O.T. do we find a religious question discussed with such a combination of penetration and piety. The way in which the proposition is set forth, that to be human is to be a sinner, betokens, not the spinning of a theory, but the testimony of one who knows the bitterness of inner conflict and is trying to convey to his reader, by means of a very simple story, the momentous nature of the inescapable urge towards self-knowledge. Why then, has it been left to man to decide for or against God? To this final question, though it is fully in line with the insight of such a keen observer, our author gives no answer. In this silence lies his religion.

II. THE DOCTRINE OF SIN
IN THE SEPTUAGINT [1]

THEOLOGICALLY important renderings in the LXX are partly due to misunderstanding and the difficulty of the Hebrew, but partly also to the intention of the translator. In Ps. cxxix (cxxviii), 3, "plowers" (*hor͏eshim*) is changed to "wicked" (*har͏esha῾im*) under the influence of the following verse; and "furrows" (*ma῾͏anoth*) to "iniquity" (ἀνομία),[2] as frequently in the LXX, abandoning the metaphor. Another case of the latter is found at Deut. xxix, 19 (18), where the Hebrew says, "to sweep away the moist with the dry". The other Greek versions retain this, but the LXX gives the meaning of the metaphor: "that the sinner may not involve the guiltless in ruin with himself". Similarly, in Ps. cxli (cxl), 5, for Heb. "oil upon the head let not my head refuse", LXX has "let not the oil of a sinner anoint my head" (changing *ro'sh* to *rasha῾*), and thus turns it into a warning against fellowship with sinners.[3]

Presumptuousness is a frequent characteristic of the sinner in the LXX. Thus ἁμαρτωλός is the rendering of *zedh* (presumptuous) at Ecclus. xi, 9, and *zadhon* at xv, 7, giving a religious turn to what is secular in the Hebrew (cf. Ps. i, 1). R. Smend's emendation

[1] For a general survey of LXX usage, see pp. 1 ff., 47 f. Here we are concerned with the theology of the Greek O.T. with respect to sin.

[2] Perhaps regarding the Hebrew as a derivative of *'anah* Pi῾el (oppress)?

[3] So A. Bertholet in Kautzsch II, 1923, 269; Gunkel emends Heb. after LXX.

33

of Ecclus. iii, 27 (*mithholel* for *mithḥolel*) would involve
the same idea of sin,[1] which also appears at Ecclus.
v, 4 f. (cf. x, 12 f.). See also Ecclus. xxxii, 12, where
the LXX ("sin not by proud speech") does not
correspond to the Hebrew ("in the fear of God and
not without understanding").[2] The tendency towards uniformity shows itself when ἁμαρτωλός is used
for "Belial" (Ecclus. xi, 32), "men of violence"
(xv, 12), "injustice" (xvi, 13), and ὁδὸς ἁμαρτίας for
"stumbling-block" (xlvii, 23).

Wealth and power are commonly regarded in O.T.
and N.T. as marks of a sinner (cf. Eccles. ii, 26;
Prov. xxiii, 17). This forces its way into Hab. iii, 14,
where *ro'sh p°razaw* is translated into τοὺς ἀρχηγοὺς
τῶν ἁμαρτωλῶν [LXX, 23, 62, 86, 147].

Sin is disease. This familiar O.T. idea leads to the
rendering of *ḥºli* by ἁμαρτία in Is. liii, 4, which is
thus made to anticipate ver. 12. The remarkable
rendering of Symmachus seems to be based on the
N.T. programme of Messianic suffering, which is
drawn from the LXX : ὄντως τὰς ἁμαρτίας ἡμῶν
αὐτὸς ἀνέλαβε καὶ τοὺς πόνους ὑπέμεινεν, ἡμεῖς δὲ
ἐλογισάμεθα αὐτὸν ἐν ἀφῇ ὄντα, πεπληγότα ὑπὸ θεοῦ
καὶ τεταπεινωμένον. According to Procopius of Gaza,
Aquila and Theodotion had the same reading.
The equation of sin with disease leads naturally to
the healing of sin at Deut. xxx, 3 ("Yahwe, thy God,
will turn thy fortune") : whereas Aquila translates
literally, and Symmachus drags in a reference to the
history of redemption [as A.V. and R.V.],[3] the LXX
quite independently, from the point of view of its
special interest in sin, introduces the idea of forgive-

[1] Die Weisheit des Jesus Sirach erklärt, 1906, 32.
[2] Smend, 290 f.
[3] So Theod., but without σοι ; Aq., Sym. and Theod. are
re-translated by Field after Masius.

ness : "the Lord will heal thy sins" (ἰάσεται κύριος
τὰς ἁμαρτίας σου). Aquila and the LXX here derive
sh*ebhuth* from *shubh* (so also Symmachus at Jer. xxxiii,
26), while Symmachus and Theodotion think of
shabhah as the LXX usually does. The LXX's
negative understanding of sh*ebhuth* is important for
the development of the idea of sin. The same thing
occurs at Ezek. xvi, 53, where the rendering is
ἀποστροφή (" apostasy "). This last word represents
m*eshubhah* four times in Jer. (v, 6 ; viii, 5 ; at vi, 19,
and xviii, 12, misread for *mahsh*ebhoth*). The context
at Jer. xiv, 7 justifies ἁμαρτία for m*eshubhah*. The LXX
thus frequently takes sh*ebhuth* and m*eshubhah* in the
negative sense of apostasy, which, according to Deut.
xxx, 3 and Jer. xiv, 7 is the fundamental sin, for which
redemption and healing are expected and prayed for
above all else. More frequently, however, the LXX
seems to avoid translating the formula, *shubh sh*ebhuth*.
This happens at Job xlii, 10, partly perhaps because
attention is directed less to the restoration of Job's
former wealth than to the friends' sin in bringing
false charges against him (ver. 8 : κατά ; cf. Ps. cix
(cviii), 6 and see p. 37). The LXX is here emphasis-
ing the forgiveness of sin, which is only hinted at in
the Hebrew. [See note on p. 38.]

Anthropomorphism finds expression in the Hebrew of
Job xlii, 7 (" my wrath is kindled against thee "),
but the LXX avoids this (ἥμαρτες σύ), as it does by
its paraphrase in ver. 9, and by its addition at the
end of ver. 10. (῎Ελυσεν τὴν ἁμαρτίαν in ver. 9 could
be justified by fact that *nasa'* is a technical term for the
forgiveness of sin. Cf. Is. i, 14 for another example.) [1]
Similarly, at Numb. i, 53, ἁμάρτημα stands for " wrath "

[1] Aq. and Sym., followed by Jerome in the Vulg., had a
literal translation. Cf. also the LXX addition, τὰς ἁμαρτίας
ὑμῶν, at Is. lv, 7.

(*qeçeph*). Instead of speaking theologically (Rom. i, 18), but still anthropomorphically—of the wrath of God which the community might incur, the LXX speaks psychologically of the sin which it should avoid. According to the Syro-Hexaplar, Symmachus has ὀργή and Theodotion θυμός, translating literally. The same kind of change is seen at Is. lvii, 17, where *qaçaphti* becomes ἐλύπησα αὐτόν. As a punishment for sin, God sends " sorrow unto repentance " (II Cor. vii, 9 f.). It is interesting to compare this with I Esdr. vi, 15 (14), where the Greek avoids the attribution of the emotion of anger to God (παραπικραίνω without object is intransitive), and introduces the word " sin ", although II Esdr. v, 12, follows the Aramaic of Ezra [see R.V.m. on Ezra iv, 8].

Idolatry. The verb *ma'al* (" act unfaithfully ") becomes ἁμαρτάνειν at II Chron. xii, 2, and ἀφίστημι at 7, the latter in accordance with the Chronicler's view of the sin of apostasy (cf. Judg. x, 10). I Esd. viii, 89, also has ἁμαρτάνειν for *ma'al*, though the corresponding passage, II Esdr. x, 2, has ἀσυνθετεῖν, which occurs six times for *ma'al*, meaning breach of the covenant with God (cf. ver. 3). The same thought is expressed at Nahum iii, 6, where for Heb. " and make thee vile " LXX has κατὰ τὰς ἁμαρτίας σου, connecting it with the word *nabhluth*. B here reads ἀκαθαρσίας, which is LXX for *nabhluth* at Hos. ii, 12 (the only place where it occurs), and is a technical term in the LXX for the sin of idolatry ; in Prov. it is used more in a psychological and ethical sense to translate *to'ebhah*, a cultic term commonly applied to idols. A's reading of ἁμαρτία for *to'ebhah* at Ezek. viii, 6, and xvi, 51, is preferable to B's conventional ἀνομία. In both cases the sin of idolatry is meant —deserting Yahwe to play the harlot (Ezek. xvi, 41 ff.). The Hebrew root *tame'*, generally translated ἀκαθαρσία

or μαίνειν, means cultic uncleanness. LXX at Lev.
xiv, 19, which speaks of the uncleanness of a leper,
purposely substitutes the moral and religious idea of
sin for the cultic.[1]

That *folly is sin* and wisdom piety, is a familiar
thought in the O.T. Perhaps that explains the use
of both ἁμαρτία and κακία for the Hebrew *'iwweleth*
at Prov. xxvi, 11 ; it often indicates culpable ignorance of God, and so godlessness. The Wisdom literature and the Law generally teach that lack of knowledge means sin ; e.g. Prov. xxiv, 9 : Aquila and
Theodotion follow the Hebrew, but LXX has ἀπο-
θνήσκει δε ἄφρων ἐν ἁμαρτίαις. (reading *zimmath* as
muth, as it does with *zimmoth* in ver. 8).

Whether purposely or by mistake, LXX (B) puts
ἁμάρτημα for *pegha'* at I Kings v, 4 (Heb. 18), and
ἁμαρτάνειν for *p°gho*ᵃ' at I Sam. xxii, 17 (AB) for
ἀπάντημα and ἀπαντᾶν ; in the former case the sin is
something which hinders the holy work of building
the Temple, as at I Chron. xxii, 8. LXX also introduces the idea of sin at Is. lxvi, 4, indicating the
reason for punishment (" I will requite their sins "),
whereas the Hebrew only mentions the punishment
(" I will bring their fears upon them "). Here again
the sin is idolatrous apostasy. Similarly at Is. xxiv, 6,
LXX has " because its inhabitants have sinned "
instead of Hebrew " are found guilty ".

A *deeper sense of sin* is reached by the LXX in Ps.
cxl, 8 (cxxxix, 9), when it turns " Grant not the
desire of the wicked " (cf. Symmachus) into " Deliver
me not up to the sinner through my own lust ".
Cf. Ps. cix (cviii), 6, where ἁμαρτωλός and διάβολος
have a metaphysical reference, not in the Hebrew,
comparable with II Thess. ii, 3. A spiritual emphasis

[1] Cf. the relation of sickness to sin in the N.T. : Mark ii, 5 ;
John v, 14 ; viii, 11.

is seen at Ezek. xxiii, 49, where "thoughts" is substituted for "idols". According to Jer. l (xxvii), 7, the enemies of the Jews excuse themselves on the ground that the Jews have sinned; LXX μὴ ἀνῶμεν αὐτούς ἀνθ' ὧν ἥμαρτον suggests, on the contrary, that they are carrying out the will of God. "Are the consolations of God too small for thee?" says Eliphaz at Job xv, 11; LXX changes this to "Thou hast received but little chastisement for thy sins", introducing the idea of suffering as education, so dear to Hellenistic Judaism. This implies a very strong sense of sin, necessitating confession. Thus, e.g., at Ecclus. iv, 26, LXX departs from Heb. "turn from sin", and says "confess thy sins".[1] Correspondingly, the hope of divine grace finds expression: where the destruction of heathen altars is called the full fruit of the putting away of sin (Is. xxvii, 9), LXX says, "This is his blessedness, when I remove his sin".

LXX thus presents a consistent linguistic usage, which points to a principle of unity in its doctrine. Instead of splitting up human sinfulness into all sorts of separate sins, after the manner of late Judaism, it shows a tendency to go to the root of the matter, to that fundamental sin which separates man from God and is indomitable (Ecclus. xxi, 2; xxvii, 10) until he lets God save him.

[*Note.*—In a communication of 14. 2. 1950 Dr. Bertram says that in his first draft he drew attention to LXX omission of verses applying the promise of *shubh shᵉbhuth* to Gentiles at Jer. xlviii, 47; xlix, 6, comparing this with LXX removal of the universalistic tone from Isaiah xix, 25.]

[1] [But see Oesterley, C.B., *ad loc.*]

III. THE JEWISH IDEA OF SIN [1]

1. THE *Law* determines the conception of sin in Judaism. Since all its provisions reveal the will of God, including what we call civil and criminal law, every kind of transgression is sin, and falls within the sphere of religion, as rebellion against God, along with specifically religious offences and cases of ceremonial carelessness. [2]

Taking over the O.T. idea that the constitutive element in sin is offence against God, Judaism shows two opposing tendencies. On the one hand scribal casuistry regards all breaches of the Law, however trivial, as sin; [3] and on the other hand an effort is made to maintain the O.T. differentiation between "sinning with a high hand" and sinning through ignorance. On the basis of Lev. xvi, 21, three kinds of sin are named at Sifra Lev. xvi, 6: unashamed misdeeds ('*awonoth*); acts of rebellion (*pish'eyhem*); unwitting offences (*hatt'otham*: cf. Tos. Yoma 2, 1; Bab. Yoma 36*b*). [4] Knowledge of the Law is here the criterion. Bab. Baba Metzia 33*b* says that, at Is. lviii, 1, "my people" means those familiar with

[1] Cf. G. F. Moore, Judaism I, 461. Tos. Shebuoth, iii, 6.

[2] The juristic idea of crime or transgression is not yet separated from the religious idea of sin. This separation is only tentative in later Judaism, the reason for this being that the O.T. is the very Word of God in its legislation as well as in its religious authority.

[3] E.g. Shab. xii, 3 ff. : "He who writes two letters (on the Sabbath), . . . is guilty ; he who writes on his body is guilty. If one writes with a liquid other than ink, or on any thing which does not preserve the writing, he is free " ; cf. Schürer II, 471 ff. ; Shebuoth i, 2-ii, 5. [4] Cf. Moore I, 464.

the Law, " whose unconscious mistakes are equivalent
to deliberate sins ", and " the house of Jacob " the
unlearned masses, " whose deliberate sins are equivalent to unconscious mistakes ".[1] The tendency to
differentiate leads, as in O.T., to the singling out of
the deadly sins : idolatry, unchastity, bloodshed.
These must never be committed.[2] The worst of all
sins is idolatry (*ªbhodhah zarah*). " It is the very
essence of rebellion, violating not only the first commandment of the Decalogue—Thou shalt have no
other Gods before me—but the fundamental principle
of the divine unity, the profession of faith solemnly
pronounced by the Jew every time he repeated the
Shema'." [3] To commit idolatry means to commit all
sins (Sifre Numb. 111 on xv, 22). Other sins can
be atoned for by [4] purification rites, good works,[5] or
sufferings,[6] but death [7] is the only atonement for the
deadly sins (Bab. Sanh. 74a).

2. Viewing sin from the standpoint of the Law,
Judaism tended to dissociate it from the community
and to fix the burden of it upon the individual. This
tendency begins in Ezekiel with the rejection of the
idea that guilt can be passed on from father to son—
as expressed in the proverb about fathers eating sour

[1] Cf. also Bab. Taanith 11a.

[2] Cf. the discussion of the Rabbis in conference at Lydda
during the persecution of Hadrian, and the decision that life
must not be purchased at the price of committing one of these
sins (Jer. Sanh. 21b ; Bab. Sanh. 74 ; Moore, I, 467). Cf.
also the apostolic decree, Acts xv, 29, and the discussion.

[3] Moore, I, 466.   [4] Cf. Moore, I, 497 ff.

[5] Cf. A. Schlatter, Jochanan ben Zakkai, 1899, 39 ff., esp. 41 :
" Trusting that the gift would earn forgiveness as its reward ".

[6] Cf. W. Wichmann, Die Leidenstheologie, 1930.

[7] See p. 39, n. 2. When a man is condemned to death under
the Jewish law, i.e. under the Torah, that is not only punishment
for the crime which he has committed—idolatry, bloodshed,
unchastity, etc.—but also atonement for his sin.

grapes and their sons' teeth being set on edge—and
the assertion of the fundamental principle : " The
soul that sinneth, it shall die " (Ezek. xviii, 2-4).
Sin is the actual transgression of the Law by the
individual, for whom it has consequences in this
world and in the world to come. The Law, the
theory of rewards and punishments, and the idea of
sin, form an indissoluble unity. This abolition of the
connexion between the sins of fathers and the fate of
their sons finds expression at two places in the Targum,
where the words of the second Commandment,
" visiting the sins of the fathers upon the children,
upon the third and upon the fourth generation ",
are changed into " inflicting punishment for the guilt
of wicked fathers upon their disobedient children "
(Exod. xx, 5), and—still more clearly ". . . when
the children follow after their fathers in sinning "
(Deut. v, 9).[1] Yet the idea of universal responsibility for sin is not quite dead. This comes out in
the parable which likens the sinner to a man boring
a hole in a boat at sea. When asked what he was
doing, he replied to his fellow-passengers, " What has
that to do with you ? May I not bore under myself ? "
Their answer was, " It is our business : the water is
pouring in, and we shall all be drowned " (Lev.
Rabba 4 on iv, 1).[2]

Generally speaking, Judaism takes the view that
sin is universal.[3] " All that are born are defiled with
iniquities, and are full of sins and laden with offences :
and if after death we were not to come into judgment,
peradventure it had been better for us " (II Esdr.
vii, 68 R.V.) ; " We that have received the Law
shall perish by sin, and our heart also which received

[1] L. Baeck in R.G.G.[2], V, 883.
[2] Cf. Moore, I, 471.
[3] Cf. Weber, 233 f. ; Str.-Bill. III, 155 ff.

it " (ix, 36). Cf. Exod. Rabba 31 (beginning) on
xxii, 24 ; Lev. Rabba 14 on xii, 2 (on Ps. li, 7) :
" Even in the most pious there must be a trace of
guilt somewhere " ; Philo, Vit. Mos. II, 147 : " sin
is innate in every man " ; Philo, De fug. et inv., 158.
The heathen also fall under this judgment as sinners
before God from the religious point of view, for,
according to Jewish theory, they have the command-
ments of Adam and Noah concerning robbery, unchastity, idolatry, blasphemy and bloodshed (Sifra Lev.
xviii, 4), and refused the Torah when it was offered
to them. Rabbi Jochanan said, " The meaning of
Deut. xxxiii, 2 and Hab. iii, 3 is that God passed the
Law round among all the nations and tongues, but
none accepted it until he came to Israel ; she accepted it " (Bab. Ab. Zar. 2b).[1] Therefore they are
not guiltless in their sin.

The doctrine of universal guilt was, however, not
carried quite as far as the above statement might seem
to suggest. A few exceptions are allowed at II Esdr.
vii, 48 R.V. Men of outstanding godliness, like
Abraham, Moses or Elijah, are accounted sinless
(Test. Zeb., 1 ; Jos. Ant. vii, 153 ; Pesiqta 76a ed.
Buber).[2] The possibility of sinlessness rests on the
freedom of the individual will and the gift of the Law.
A clean life is made possible by observing the Law.
" God said to the Israelites, My children, I have
created in you the evil inclination ; I have also
created for you the Law as a means of salvation ; so
long as you occupy yourselves with the latter, the
former will have no power over you " (Sifre Deut. 45
on xi, 18). These ideas form the background of
Paul's assertion, " As touching the righteousness

[1] Cf. Str.-Bill. III, 38-43. See II Esdr. vii, 20-24 [and
Ecclus. xxiv, 5-8].
[2] Weber, 53 ff., 224.

which is in the Law, found blameless " (Phil. iii, 6).[1]
If sinlessness is attributed to certain godly men, being
made possible by observance of the Law, it follows
that it will be predicated of the Messiah. Already of
the Servant of the Lord it had been said, " He had
done no violence, neither was any deceit in his mouth "
(Is. liii, 9). Ps. Sol. xvii, 41 says of the Messiah,
" He shall be free from sin ", and Test. Jud. ii, 4(A),
" No sin shall be found in him " (cf. Test. Lev. xviii,
9). Along with this goes the Jewish eschatological
expectation that sin will be removed and men will be
sinless in the Messianic Kingdom (cf. En. v, 8 f. ;
Ps. Sol. xvii, 32 ; Test. Lev. xviii).

3. The origin and the consequences of sin likewise
receive attention in post-Biblical Judaism. The question of origin receives a historical answer ; sin derives
from Adam (and Eve) and has extended its power
over the whole of mankind : " The first Adam bearing
a wicked heart transgressed and was overcome ; and
not he only, but all they also that are born of him.
Thus disease was made permanent ; and the Law was
in the heart of the people along with the wickedness
of the root ; so the good departed away, and that
which was wicked abode still " (II Esdr. iii, 21 f.).
Cf. Ecclus. xxv, 24 ; II Esdr. iii, 26 ; vii, 48 ff.,
esp. 118 ; Syr. Bar. xlviii, 42, where sin is derived
from Eve ; and esp. Syr. Bar. liv, 15 : " Though
Adam first sinned, and brought untimely death upon
all, yet of those who were born from him each one
of them hath prepared for his own soul torment to
come ".[2] Sin is here seen, as throughout the N.T.,

[1] See Aboth R. Nathan, 59, where it is said of Jochanan's
son, " He departed this life without sin ". Cf. A. Schlatter,
Jochanan b. Zakkai, 1899, 20 f.

[2] Cf. Tanchuma, Bereschith, 29, Hukkat, 39, ed. S. Buber,
for a clear expression of vexation with Adam for the trouble
he has caused by his sin.

as a power controlling this world at the deepest level.
A different account of sin's origin is found in En.
x, 4 ff. ; lxiv, 1 ff. ; Mart. Is. v, 3, where it is traced
to the fallen angels of Gen. vi. 1 ff. A more philosophical treatment of the question asserts that the
root of man's sin is the evil inclination which God
has implanted in him : Ecclus. xv, 14 ; xxxvii, 3 ;
II Esdr. iii, 20 ; iv, 4 ; vii, 48 (cor malignum) ; [1]
Pesiqta 38b-39a ed. Buber ; Vit. Ad. 19 (ἐπιθυμία
. . . ἐστὶ κεφαλὴ πάσης ἁμαρτίας).

It is the evil inclination that entices man to sin.
Man's task is to overcome this by observing the Law.
If he fails, he has to bear the consequences of sin,
which consist of all kinds of suffering. Paul's theme
in Rom. i, 18 ff.—God punishes sin with sinning—
is familiar to Judaism in the form, " sin begets sin " ;
Ps. Sol. iii, 12 says, " the sinner will add sin to sins ".
One sin, whatever it may be, leads on to another,
until the deadly sin is reached : " To-day the evil
inclination says, Do this, and to-morrow, Do that ;
until at last it says, Worship other gods, and he goes
and does it " (Bab. Shab. 105b ; cf. Ab. iv, 2 ; Sifre
Numb. 112 on xv, 30). Sin also causes separation
from God. The worship of the golden calf made it
impossible for the Israelites to see the glory of God.[2]
Sin rules out intimate intercourse with God, face to
face (cf. Exod. xxxiii, 11-23).[3] God's gracious pur-

[1] Moore, I, 479 ff. ; Weber, 221 f., 225 ff. ; F. C. Porter,
The Yeçer Hara, Yale Bibl. & Sem. Studies, 1902, 93-156 ;
A. Büchler, Studies in Sin and Atonement in the Rabb. Lit.
of the first century, 1928 ; K. Stier, Paulus üb. d. Sünde u. d.
Judentum s. Zeit, Prot. Mon. II, 1907, 104 ; Bousset-Gress-
mann, 402 ff.

[2] Cf. the exposition of Exod. xxiv, 17 and xxxiv, 30 by Simeon
b. Jochai in Sif. Numb. 1 on v, 3.

[3] Gen. iii, 8 ; Exod. xxxiv, 30 ; II Sam. xvii, 2 ; Song
iii, 7 f. ; I Sam. xxviii, 5 ; cf. Pesiqta 44b-45a (ed. Buber) and
—with a difference—Rom. iii, 23.

pose for man is thwarted again and again by sin.
This is illustrated by stories of Israel in the wilderness
(Sifre Deut. 319 ; Pesiqta 166*a-b*, Buber).

Sin is followed by punishment. The connexion
between the two is close (Ps. Sol. ii, 17 ; Philo Leg.
All. I, 35 ; Vit. Mos. I, 96 ; Sacr. A.C. 131). Sickness is a punishment for sin, and it is a recognised
formula that no man can recover from sickness until
one (i.e. God) forgives all his sins (Bab. Ned. 41*a*).
Finally, sin is punished with death and eternal damna-
tion : " No death without sin and no chastisement
without guilt " (Bab. Shab. 51*a* ; cf. Ecclus. xxv, 24 ;
Wis. i, 13 ; ii, 23 f. ; Ap. Bar. xxiii, 4 ; II Esdr. iii, 7 ;
Sifre Deut. 305 on xxxi, 14 ; Gen. Rabba xvi, 6,
near the end, where death is brought into relation
with the Fall) ; " the sinner's destruction for ever "
(Ps. Sol. iii, 13).

Nevertheless it is possible for man to repent and
return to God. This is stated with special lucidity
in the Targum of Eccles. vii, 20, where the categorical
declaration that " there is none righteous upon earth,
doing good and free from sin ", is followed by the
words, " but God shows guilty man the way of conversion before he dies ".[1]

[1] See p. 41, n. 1. With the thought of conversion a new
tendency takes its place beside the dominant tendency to
identify crime and sin, punishment and atonement, viz., the
purely religious idea of sin as something which cannot be removed by legal punishment—only a right relationship with
God can take it away (through penitence, good works, suffering,
death, or punishment by God in the world to come).

IV. GREEK USAGE

1. ἁμαρτάνειν means to fail, miss, mistake ; its synonym is ἀποτυγχάνειν (Suid.), its opposite τυγχάνειν (cf. Hom. Il., V, 287 ; Herod I, 43). From Homer onwards it is used in a concrete sense (Suid. ἄσκοπα τοξεύειν) : Plato, Hip. Min. 375a, τοῦ σκοποῦ ; Aristoph. Plut. 961, τῆς ὁδοῦ. After Herodotus it also has a transferred sense, esp. of intellectual failure : Thuc. I, xxxiii, 3 ; Philo, Omn. Prob. Lib. 133 ; hence also absolutely, of being mistaken : Dio Chrys. Or. liii, 3. The contrast to the ἁμαρτάνων is the σοφός ; the ἁμαρτίνοος is the insane : Hes. Theog. 511. But already in Homer it indicates making a mistake : Hom. Od. xxii, 154 ; Xenoph. Cyrop. V, iv, 19, τὸ γὰρ ἁμαρτάνειν ἀνθρώπους ὄντας οὐδὲν θαυμαστόν (errare humanum est). The connotation of wrong-doing in the moral sense also begins to be found : Hom. Il. IX, 501 ; Od. xiii, 214.

The LXX uses ἁμαρτάνειν occasionally for pasha', 'asham, rasha' Hiph., but mostly literally for ḥaṭa', the meaning of which developed from that of missing the way, literally and metaphorically, until it reached the connotation of going wrong morally, i.e. the dominant religious sense of sin. It was through its use for ḥeṭ' in the LXX that ἁμαρτία acquired its definitely religious content (see pp. 1 ff., 33 ff.).

2. ἁμάρτημα as a verbal noun ending in -μα denotes the occurrence of ἁμαρτάνειν, i.e. failure or blunder, suggesting foolishness or delusion rather than wickedness : Soph Ant. 1261. Aristotle defines ἁμάρτημα (Eth. Nic. V, 10, p. 1135b 18 ; Rhet. I, 13, p. 1374b 5) as coming between ἀδίκημα and ἀτύχημα : it is not

46

unexpected, but is done without malice. In common
parlance, and specially in its legal use, ἁμάρτημα more
and more indicates intentional, culpable wrong-doing :
Tebtunis Pap. v, 3 ; Antiph. i, 27 : ἑκούσια καὶ ἐκ
προνοίας ἀδικήματα καὶ ἁμαρτήματα. In the LXX
ἁμάρτημα represents mainly ḥaṭṭa'th, sometimes 'awon,
pesha', resha'. It occurs with special frequency in Wis.
(ii, 12 ; iv, 20, etc.), always with the moral and religious
connotation of a sinful action. It is coupled with
ἀδίκημα (Gen. xxxi, 36) ; ἀδικία (Deut. xix, 15 ; Jer.
xiv, 20) ; ἀσέβημα (Deut. ix, 27) ; ἀνόμημα (Josh.
xxiv, 19) ; ἀνομία (Is. lviii, 1). Further, at Is. xl, 2 it
means punishment for sin. In secular Greek it is used
more frequently than ἁμαρτία, but in Biblical usage
the latter far surpasses it, both in frequency and in
importance.

The N.T. seldom uses ἁμάρτημα to denote a sinful
action : Mark iii, 28 f. ; iv, 12 Rec. ; Rom. iii, 25 ;
v, 16 DG It. Pesh. (Sin. B : ἁμαρτήσαντος) ; I Cor.
vi, 18 ; II Pet. i, 9.

ἁμαρτία, used from the time of Aeschylus in the
metaphorical sense, like ἁμάρτημα, is often distinguished
from the latter as the quality of an action is distinguished from the action itself (Clem. Al. Strom. II,
xv, 64, 3).[2] But the distinction early tends to vanish,
since the fact of sin can only be recognised in the
sinful act. Already in Aeschylus ἁμαρτία means
wickedness (Ag, 1197 : παλαιὰς τῶνδ᾽ ἁμαρτίας δομῶν).
This word has nothing to do with the question of
guilt in the modern sense (cf. ἁμάρτημα, p. 46),
and often denotes a punishable offence committed
with a good motive, e.g. Soph. Phil. 1225 ; Trach.

[1] Cf. R. Taubenschlag, Das Strafrecht im Rechte d. Papyri,
1916, 8 ; L. Wenger, Archiv f. Pap.-forsch., 1902, 483 ; Hey,
Ἁμαρτία.
[2] Cremer-Kög., 139 ; Trench, 154 f.

483. Correspondingly, in law and philosophy it has
a wider reach ; Pseudo-Plat. Def. 416a : πρᾶξις παρὰ
τὸν ὀρθὸν λογισμόν (where ὀρθός can be taken morally,
formally, or intellectually). As the antithesis of
ὀρθότης (Plato Leg. I, 627d ; II, 668c), of course
ἁμαρτία specifies the nature of a wicked act (see
above), but more often it covers the whole proceeding,
from the evil imagination to the deed itself : Plat.
Gorg. 525c ; Aristot. Pol. IV, 16, p. 1336a, 1.

Aristotle defines ἁμαρτία as missing the mark of
virtue through lack of strength, skill, or knowledge
(Eth. Nic. II, 5, p. 1106b, 25 ff.). That means a
wrong perpetrated without malice (III, 13, p. 1118b,
16 ff. etc.), i.e. an intellectual shortcoming, that works
out morally according to the intellectual character
of Greek ethics (III, 1, p. 1110b, 18 ff.). On the
other hand, the thought of guilt, excluded by Aristotle,[1]
came later to be connected with ἁμαρτία : Pap.
Leipz. 1119, 3 ; Ditt. Syll. 3rd ed., 1042, 15.[2]

In the LXX ἁμαρτία, here practically synonymous
with ἁμάρτημα, usually stands for ḥaṭṭa'th or ḥᵃṭa'ah,
often for 'awon, sometimes for pesha', 'asham, resha'.
It was in the LXX that ἁμαρτία, like ἁμαρτάνειν,
first came to have the moral and religious quality
which it lacked both in the rapidly changing Greek
of common speech and in the " tragic " language of
Aristotle, and to indicate guilt as the outcome of an
evil will, an evil purpose, i.e. of a conscious rebellion
against God and contradiction of him (= ἀδικία).

[1] Hey shows how Ἀμαρτία became the key word in Aristotle's
teaching on drama, but was unsuitable as the starting-point for
the theory of " tragic guilt ". In view of Aristotle's exclusion
of the idea of moral guilt in the modern sense, and of its inclusion
in the Bible, Hey says that " the word ἁμαρτία thus reflects
the deep and far-reaching difference between two worlds of
culture " (163).

[2] Cf. Trench, 152.

The choice of the vaguest and most general profane word for wrong—only partly because of its kindred primary meaning—to bear the main burden of expressing the relentless Biblical idea of sin (*heṭ'*) gave it more weight than all its synonyms, and fitted it to denote the godward side of sin much better than, e.g. ἀδικία and κακία, which were primarily ethical terms.[1]

3. The N.T. follows the LXX[2] in using ἁμαρτία, etc., to denote offence against God, with the emphasis on guilt. Ἁμαρτία may be said to indicate sin in three principal forms : (*a*) a single act (= ἁμάρτημα) ; (*b*) a characteristic of human nature ; (*c*) a personal power. These lay already to hand, but their development in the N.T. (esp. (*b*) and (*c*)) betokens a doctrine different from all that went before, viz. that sin is a positive force alienating man from God.

(*a*) The reference is to sinful acts always in the Synoptic Gospels, Acts, the Pastoral Epistles, and the Apocalypse ; and generally in Heb. and the Catholic Epistles. Matt., Mark, Luke, Acts only use the word when speaking of forgiveness (except Matt. i, 21, and Mark i, 5 par.), and always in the plural (except Matt. xii, 31, and Acts vii, 60). In the case of Paul this usage generally occurs only in quotations or traditional formulae (I Cor. xv, 3 ; Gal. i, 4 ; Col. i, 14) ; exceptions are found at Rom. vii, 5 ; II Cor. xi, 7 ; Eph. ii, 1 ; apart from Rom. iv, 8 and II. Cor. xi, 7 the word is always in the plural. John uses ἁμαρτία in this sense in the Gospel only at viii, 24, twice ; viii, 34*a* ; ix, 34 (allusion to Ps. li, 5) ; on the other hand there are several examples in I John,

---

[1] Cf. Cremer-Kög., 137 f.

[2] Steinleitner (see p. 61), 85 : "The contrast between heathenism and Christianity appears nowhere more clearly than in the meanings attached to ἁμαρτία ".

which is thus seen to stand nearer to the world of
ordinary Christian thought than the Gospel.[1]

(*b*) Wrongness is what Plato means by ἁμαρτία when
he contrasts it with ὀρθότης in a discussion of the laws
of musical or poetic art (Leg. I, 627*d* ; II, 668*c*). A
complete transformation takes place when in the N.T.
it comes to mean man's inveterate hostility toward
God, specially as that is expressed in John's synonymous
formulæ : ἔχειν ἁμαρτίαν (ix, 41 ; [2] xv, 22, 24 ; xix,
11 ; I John i, 8) and ἁμαρτία ἐν τινί ἐστιν (I John
iii, 5, cf. John vii, 18). A similar expression, only
reversing the spatial relationship, is found at viii, 21 :
ἀποθανεῖν ἐν τῇ ἁμαρτίᾳ.[3] Cf. John viii, 24 (Ezek.
xviii, 24) ; ix, 34 ; I Cor, xv, 17 : apart from
Christ, man lives and dies in sins. The plural in
these passages corresponds to the collective use of
the singular in John (cf. ix, 41 ; I John i, 7) and
frequently in the Pauline and deuteroPauline literature : Rom. iii, 20 ; v, 13, 20 ; vi, 1, 6*a* ; vii, 7 ;
viii, 3 ; Heb. iv, 15 ; ix, 28, 26 ; xi, 25 ; I Pet.
iv, 1 ; and II Cor. v, 21, a specially pregnant expression for man's sinful condition as a whole.

(*c*) Personification of sin is found in the Paris
Magic Papyrus (Preisendanz, Pap. Gr. Mag. IV,
1448) : Ἁμαρτίαι χθόνιαι, underground demons ;
and also in Judaism, in Zech. v, 5 ff., the woman of

---

[1] Here also the Cognate Accusative [see A. T. Robertson,
A Grammar of the Gk. N.T.[3], 1919, 477], ἁμαρτάνω ἁμαρτίαν,
derived from LXX : Exod. xxxii, 30 f. ; Lev. iv, 23 ; v, 6, 10,
13 ; Ezek. xviii, 24 ; also Philo, De Mut. Nom. 233 ; Hermas V,
ii, 2, 4. Secular Greek prefers the more exact ἁμ. ἁμάρτημα :
Soph., Phil. 1249 ; Plato, Phaedo 113*e* ; Dio Chrys. Or. xxxii, 3.
Cf. M. Johannessohn, Der Gebrauch der Kasus u.d. Präpositionen
in d. LXX, Diss. Berlin, 1910, 56 f. ; Winer, 32, 2.

[2] Cf. Pesiqta 5 p. 55*b* Buber, in Schlatter, Johannes 232.

[3] Cf. Jer. xxxi (LXX xxxviii), 30 ; Bab. Shab. 55*b* in Schlatter,
Joh. 208.

sin,[1] and Ecclus. xxvii, 10, sin lying in wait for prey
like a lion—these being related to the gradually
developing idea of a cosmic power of evil.[2] A similar
presupposition was originally involved in the personal
treatment of ἁμαρτία (mostly with the article)[3] which
occurs frequently in the N.T., specially in Rom.
v-vii.[4] At first it is simply a matter of appearing
on the scene, as a person does (v, 12). Sin was originally dead (vii, 8), but came to life again through the
commandment of law (ver. 9), which gave it an
impulse (v. 7, 11) to deceive and entrap man
(ver. 11, cf. Heb. iii, 13 ; xii, 1). Thus, dwelling
in man (Rom. vii, 17, 20) and bringing forth passions
(ver. 5) and lust (8), sin obtains mastery over him,
as a demonic power. Man is under sin (Rom. iii, 9 ;
Gal. iii, 22 ; cf. Rom. xi, 32), as a slave (Rom. vi, 16,
20 ; John viii, 34 ; cf. Gal. ii, 17), sold to it (Rom.
vii, 14), in bondage to it (Rom. vi, 6), under its law
(vii, 23, 25 ; viii, 3), presenting parts of his body to
it as instruments of unrighteousness (vi, 13). Sin's
domain is the flesh, and its dominion (vi, 14 ; v, 21 ;
vi, 12) is consummated when it gives man death as
his wages (vi, 23 ; v, 21 ; vii, 11, cf. James i, 15).
But through and with Christ man dies to sin (Rom.
vi, 2, 10) and is dead to it (ver. 11), set free from it
(vv. 7, 18, 22), while it is condemned (viii, 3).
Nevertheless the fight against it must ever be maintained (Heb. xii, 4).

[1] Cf. R. Smend, Lehrbuch d. A.T. Rel. Gesch.[2], 1899, 402.

[2] Cf. Köberle, 473 f.

[3] Generally speaking, the presence or absence of the article,
though used, e.g. in Cremer-Kög., as a principle for the grouping
of meanings, is of little significance : cf. Rom. vi, 6 with viii, 3 ;
vi. 16 with 17 etc.

[4] Cf. Lietzmann, Röm.[2], 65 ; M. Dibelius, Die Geisterwelt
im Glaube d. Paulus, 1909, 119 ff. ; P. Feine, Theol. d. N.T.[5],
1931, 200 f.

It is difficult to decide how much of this to regard, with Dibelius, as referring to the demon, Sin, playing the part of Satan in Rom. vi f., and how much, with Feine, as mere poetic imagery.   How fluid the boundaries are between these N.T. forms of the conception of sin is well illustrated in the Johannine literature : cf. John viii, 34 ; I John iii, 5 ; John viii, 21 and 24.

V. SIN AND GUILT IN CLASSICAL GREEK AND HELLENISM

1. THE Christian idea of sin is not found in classical Greek literature, which knows nothing of the hostility to God that excludes what is right from thought and will.[1] In this chapter, therefore, we shall do well to avoid that idea, and substitute the Greek conception of failure and guilt, adhering to the fundamental meaning of ἁμαρτάνειν, etc., which is to miss the mark—whether through error or guilt, or error that is guilt.

The field is wide, extending from crime to trivial blundering,[2] and includes moral lapses as well as intellectual or artistic mistakes—even in the writings of a single author.[3] Ἁμαρτάνειν had become a purely negative term for doing what is, not ὀρθόν, i.e. customary or conventional, or logically or technically correct.[4]

A full treatment of this Greek idea of guilt is not possible without reference to certain other ideas and terms ; e.g. ἄτη for the early period, combining fate and freedom,[5] and ἀδικία, etc., for post-Homeric

---

[1] Kierkegaard, The Sickness unto Death, trans. W. Lowrie, Princeton, 1941, 153 : " Sin does not consist in the fact that man has not understood what is right, but in the fact that he will not understand it, and in the fact that he will not do it." See the whole chapter (141 ff.), The Socratic definition of sin, which analyses the Greek and Christian ideas of sin. [See also A. W. Mair in E.R.E. XI, 545-554 ; R. Livingstone, The Greek Genius.] [2] Hey, 14.

[3] Cf. the large number of examples in Hey, 7 ff., esp. from Thucydides and the law-courts (14 f.) and from Aristotle (141 ff.).

[4] Hey, 15 f.

[5] Cf. W. Jaeger, Solons Eunomie, Sitz. Akad. Berl., 1926.

times. Hesiod's own personal experience led him to
base everything in the " Works " on the conviction
that all injustice is sin.[1] Since community life is
impossible without justice, ἀδικία came to mean
simply departure from the norm of ordinary life.
Other terms to be noted are ἅγος and μίασμα, denoting ritual pollution, ὕβρις (insolence), and κακός,
κακία, specially in philosophical literature.

2. Greek life in the earliest days was a glad accept-
ance of whatever came from fate and the gods, without
any fully developed self-consciousness or sense of
personal freedom, and this determined the conception
of guilt (cf. Homer, Il. xix, 83 ff.)[2] It was misfortune that drew attention to the fact that guilt had
been incurred. Guilt or failure is a matter of behaviour. In the Homeric age it consists of negligence
in worship, false witness, breach of the laws of hospital-
ity, offence against the honour (τιμή) of gods and
men. Hesiod widens the circle, so as to include the
injuring or dishonouring of parents, adultery, ill-
treatment of orphans and social injustice in general
(Works 327 ff.). Such things call forth the anger of
the gods, who are the guardians and guarantors of
law and order. Cf. Homer, Od. xiii, 214 : " Zeus
. . . watches over all men and punishes the transgressor ". Rohde's remark about the Greek spirit in
its spring-time is broadly true : " In those happy
centuries they were practically free from that in-
fectious disease, the consciousness of sin ".[3]

3. The Homeric world of the seventh and sixth
centuries B.C. was inundated with oriental morbidity,
and the Greeks began to see life in terms of guilt
and death ;[4] behind the familiar light of day they

---

[1] Latte, 266. [2] Cf. esp. Stenzel (see Bibliogr.), 17 ff.
[3] Rohde, Psyche [9], [10], 1925, I, 319.
[4] Cf. H. Weinstock, Sophokles 275 ff., esp. 279 f.

began to sense "the dark backward and abysm of time", [1] to doubt the reality of their existence, to tremble at fate, to feel that guilt is inescapable. Everywhere men sought refuge from their fears in the Mysteries, and specially in Orphism. The new doctrine was that life itself is the consequence of guilt. "The soul is condemned to life in the body for the expiation of guilt ; the wages of sin is life on earth, which is death to the soul." [2]   Man's chief concern is with the "original guilt" which precedes life, and the judgment of the dead which follows it ;[3] and these are elaborated in art and philosophy. The way in which the Greeks met the menace of all this deepened and enriched their spiritual life. "Tragic drama is the visible and abiding proof that the Greek spirit transformed the menace into a blessing." [4]   Whereas formerly the guilt was seen in the deed itself, now it was recognised as a deeply rooted condition of the inner man (see p. 57).

Human guilt is disturbance of the established order, interference with an objective state of affairs, for which man has to pay with the consequent suffering and misery, and sometimes with death. It has not the moral quality of a free choice between good and evil, but is an infatuation concurrent with life itself.[5]   Man is doomed to incur guilt. The idea of ἄγνοια (ignorance), which plays such an important part in the Greek view of life, here reaches its deepest level.

[1] Weinstock, 280.   [2] Rohde II, 126.
[3] Cf. Latte, 281 ff., for evidence.   [4] Weinstock, 280.
[5] Cf. the scene in Sophocles, Antigone, in which Creon comes out of the house with Haemon's body :—Chorus : "Evidence he with him bears against himself;" Creon : "Woe for sin of minds perverse, deadly fraught with mortal curse. . . . Heavy the hand of God, thorny and rough the paths my feet have trod" (1258 ff). Shortly before this Teiresias had said : "To err is common to all men" (1023 f.). [Trans. F. Storr in Loeb ed.]

All guilt springs from ignorance, but this is conceived
as the limitation of man's powers without which he
would not be human. The deep meaning of the
Oedipus tragedy, e.g. is to be found in " the tragic
limitation of human knowledge, which as such is
necessarily fragmentary ", and which " gives men's
actions their tragic quality, since they cannot be
actions in the full sense unless they are consciously
directed towards an object and arise out of clear
knowledge ".[1] Thus " all action involves guilt, since
it affects the course of things in the continuum of
space and time, the agent, in his ignorance, being
neither able to foresee the results nor ultimately
responsible for them ".[2] The only thing man can do
is to shoulder his guilt,[3] as, e.g. Oedipus does, accept-
ing his guilt and his doom from the hand of the gods,[4]
and acknowledging guilt when his suffering comes.
This suffering contains the final secret of man's life
and of all existence. Like everything else, human
guilt is taken up into the will and decree of the gods.
By incurring guilt and reaping its bitter fruit, the
Greeks felt that they were brought to a deeper understanding of the world (Aeschylus, Agam. 176 f.).
That is Greek religion.

The idea of guilt as inseparable from human action
made it possible to conceive of voluntary guilt, like
that confessed by Prometheus in the famous tragedy
of Aeschylus (259 ff.). The Chorus says, " Seest thou
not thou hast erred ? Yet to say how thou didst,
can bring to me no joy, and to thee pain " ; to which

[1] Weinstock, 151 ; cf. 172 ff., 230 ff.   [2] *Ibid.* 175.
[3] Cf. further the analysis of Ajax in W. Schadewalt, Sophokles
Aias und Antigone, in " Neue Wege zur Antike ", 8, 1929,
70 ff., esp. what is said in the closing section on " greatness
and guilt " (100 ff.).
[4] Cf. Oedipus Col. 974 : " And if when born to misery, as
born I was ".

the hero replies, " Wilfully I erred, wilfully ; I deny not ; succouring mortals, I reaped woes myself." [Trans. by R. C. Trevelyan.] This is the existential guilt which conditions the human situation and involves it in suffering.

The tragedians' ideas of existential guilt is closely connected with a late Homeric development, as seen in the well-known passage (Od. i, 32 ff.) where Zeus says, " Lo you now, how vainly mortal men do blame the gods! For of us they say comes evil, whereas they even of themselves, through the blindness of their own hearts, have sorrows beyond that which is ordained." [Trans. Butcher and Lang.] In the midst of that suffering which is the inescapable doom of a guilt that is also doomed, there is another kind of misery, self-inflicted, when a man incurs guilt in spite of divine warning of the fatal consequences of wrong-doing : " With sheer doom before his eyes, since he had warned him " (Hom. Od. i, 37 ff.). This is the first indication of insight into the operation of immanent laws which are clearly discernible, " the laws ", as Solon later calls them, " of evolving reality, according to which justice is done in every age, so that evil is defeated and good victorious ".[1] The ignorance which leads to guilt is here the lack of the knowledge of what is good, i.e. of what leads to happiness by the very working of these laws. Philosophy developed these ideas. Democritus had already said that " the cause of sin is ignorance (ἀμαθίη) of the better way " (Fr. 83, Diels II, 78, 13). Socrates based his work as an educator on the fundamental principle that ignorance is the ground of guilt and evil. The Greek philosophers took it for granted that right understanding leads to right action, the reference

[1] Stenzel, 27 after Fr. 3, 30 ff. (Diehl I, 24) ; 24, 3 (I, 35) ; 10 (I, 28 f.).

being to existential insight and not to mere intellectual
knowledge.   He who really understands and knows [1]
will act rightly.   The theory rests on the belief that
man is fundamentally good.[2]   Greek tragedy starts
from this idea of insight as determining action : it is
animated " by belief in a comprehensible, unified
world-order, in which we may expect wickedness and
presumption to meet with their deserts, and so regulate
our behaviour according to the obvious relation between guilt and punishment, gaining insight through
the great examples of suffering in mythology or
through our own experience " ; [3] and it also stands in
a vital relation to the idea of the city-state.[4]   Along

---

[1] Cf. Kierkegaard on the inner dialectic of this Socratic theory
of ignorance : " When a person doesn't do the right thing ;
why then, neither has he understood it ; his understanding is a
vain conceit, his assertion that he has understood it is a false
indication of the way. . . . But then indeed the definition is
correct.   If a man does the right thing, then surely he doesn't
sin ; and if he doesn't do the right thing, then neither has he
understood it ; if in truth he had understood it, this would at
once have moved him to do it, would at once make him an echo
of his understanding—*ergo*, sin is ignorance."   (Trans. W. Lowrie,
149 f.)

[2] Kierkegaard shows that the Socratic definition of sin is no
definition.   " If the Socratic definition is correct, sin does not
exist " (144).   He also brings out the point that the Greeks
believed man to be naturally good, when he asks pertinently,
" What determinant is it then that Socrates lacks in determining
what sin is ? " and replies, " It is will, defiant will."   The Greek
intellectualism was too happy, too naïve, too aesthetic, too
ironical, too witty, [too sinful] to be able to get it into its head
that a person knowingly could fail to do the good, or knowingly,
with knowledge of what was right, do what was wrong.   The
Greek spirit proposes an intellectual categorical imperative "
(145).   [3] Stenzel, 87.

[4] Stenzel (84-87) analyses Aeschylus, Eumenides, and shows
that the ordering of the state is a divine ordering : " The doctrine
of the immanence of the supernatural in the natural, at which
philosophy arrived after long and painful wrestling, was antici-
pated by the poet ".

with this, it is true, goes the idea of existential guilt
(see p. 55), which can over-ride all insight, for guilt
is fore-doomed and ignorance is an infatuation (ἄτη).
But both lines of thought come together in the moral
underlying Tragedy, which reveals the part played by
ignorance and teaches reverence for the divine omnis-
cience.[1]   Plato's ideas about guilt find their fullest
expression in what he says about unrighteousness
(ἀδικία), which is identical with sin (ἁμαρτία)—cf.
e.g. Gorg. 525c ; Phaed. 113e ; Laws X, 906c—and
about evil (κακόν). He takes the opposite view of the
connexion between guilt and destiny, echoing Homer,
Od. I, 32 ff. : man chooses his own lot. He alone is
guilty, and God has no responsibility (Rep. X, 617e).
Aristotle makes a sharp new distinction between ἁμαρτία
and ἀδικία.[2]   " I mean by an accident (ἀτύχημα)
anything which cannot be foreseen and does not
proceed from vice, by an error (ἁμάρτημα) anything
which might have been foreseen and yet does not
proceed from wickedness, and by a crime (ἀδίκημα)
anything which might have been foreseen and is itself
a result of wickedness " (Rhet. I, 13, p. 1374b, 7 ff.,
Welldon).   What sort of " errors " are meant here ?
The word-group to which ἁμαρτία belongs is widely
used, indicating error in the fields of art and thought,[3]
technique and hygiene,[4] law and its administration,[5]
and politics.[6] Finally, in the sphere of ethics, ἁμαρτία
means an error committed in good faith, the result
of ignorance to which no blame attaches.   Virtue is

---

[1] Cf. the end of Sophocles, Oedipus Tyr. : " Therefore wait
to see Life's ending ere thou count one mortal blest ; wait till
free from pain and sorrow he has gained his final rest " [Storr].
Note also how the idea of an immanent law appears again in
the revelations of the oracle (see Weinstock's interpretation,
op. cit., 184 ff.).

[2] Cf. esp. Hey, 137 ff.   [3] Hey, 141.
[4] Hey, 141 f.   [5] Hey, 143.   [6] Hey, 145.

for Arisotle the mean between two extremes, and ἁμαρτία means going astray to right or left : [1] " There are many ways of going wrong (ἁμαρτάνειν) . . ., but only one of keeping straight ; . . . it is easy to miss the mark but hard to reach it " (Eth. Nic. II, 5, p. 1106*b*, 28 ff.). Error in every sphere is the result of ignorance (for ethics see Eth. Eud. VIII, 1, p. 1246*a*, 32 ff. ; Pol. III, 11, p. 1231*b*, 28) ; every trace of moral responsibility has disappeared ; for Aristotle it is all a matter of the intellect.[2] This belongs to the rationalism of Aristotle and his successors.

4. The two lines of thought, which had been held together by the theories of ignorance and immanence, now fell apart : on the one hand existential guilt, foredoomed, and on the other hand error, due to ignorance and causing suffering. Philosophy continues to be rationalistic. All guilt comes from ignorance, which is to be removed by education. Man is naturally good, and realises goodness through the exercise of reason. " Error (τὸ ἁμαρτάνειν) comes from not knowing how to decide what ought to be done " (Clem. Al., Strom. II, 15, 62, 3 ; cf. Epict. Diss. I, 26, 6). Thus the philosophy of the later period lost the serious view of guilt which had prevailed in the classical age.[3]

But the thought of doom maintained itself. No

---

[1] Hey, 147 ff., with full evidence.

[2] Hey, 160 ; cf. 161 : " We have no expression exactly corresponding to the Greek word, ἁμαρτία, with all its varied nuances ; it is for us an ἀνώνυμον, to use Aristotle's term. We can use such renderings as mistake, blunder, miscalculation, error, slip, wrong inference, misunderstanding, perversity, folly—but not lapse or transgression—according to the nature and gravity of each instance."

[3] A recovery of the conception of sin is not to be thought of : sin—" the word really has no place in the Stoic system " (Bonhöffer).

longer rising to the same height by identifying guilt
with fate, it robbed man of responsibility by making
him the plaything of chance.[1]   The Mystery religions,
which invaded the Greek world in increasing numbers
in the Hellenistic period, aimed at counteracting the
curse of doom and mortality.   Similarly the Hellenistic mysticism of the Corpus Hermeticum sees the
world as the domain of cosmic evil and man as the
victim of vice from which only the free gift of Gnosis
can save him.   Ignorance and Gnosis are metaphysical opposites.   The prevalence of the idea of
fate weakened the sense of personal responsibility :
" Chance . . . made man sin, in spite of his reason "
(Libanius, Ep. 1025).   It makes no difference whether
a man has knowledge or not ; his guilt is predestined,
like the rest of his existence.   The terms ἁμαρτία, etc.,
consequently have a different connotation :   " Euer-
getes II's peace proclamation shows how far the intellectual colouring of the word ἁμαρτάνειν had been lost
when it makes ἁμαρτήματα complementary to ἀγνοήματα,
in order to include all offences in one expression."[2]
Ἁμαρτάνειν is now the universal lot of mankind.[3]

5. Steinleitner's collection of Phrygian and Lydian
inscriptions lies outside the main stream of Greek
and Hellenistic thought.[4]   The primitive religions
which they represent show the god as the absolute
lord of those who worship him, benevolent towards
them, and himself punishing every offence.   Sin is

[1] [Cf. Polybius i, 4 :   " It is my task as an historian to put
before my readers a compendious view of the part played by
Fortune in bringing about the general catastrophe. . . . She
is constantly producing dramas in the life of men."]

[2] Pap. Tebt. I, v, 3 (Latte).

[3] " No man can live without sin " (F. Preisigke, Sammelbuch,
4949, 17 ff ; 5716, 17).

[4] F. S. Steinleitner, Die Beicht im Zusammenhange m.d.
sakralen Rechtspflege in d. Antike (Diss. München, 1913).

offence against the deity, whether conscious and intentional or unconscious and unintentional ; its religious character is seen when it is equated with despising the god.[1] Sin includes refusal to give thanks to the god, insulting speech, breach of purity rules, damage to the shrine, neglect of the demand for ritual chastity, mistakes in ritual, and perjury.[2] A number of the sins mentioned are ethical in character. The god reacts against every sin with a particular punishment. Sickness is specially regarded as a punishment for sin, which is actually called a "substance begetting sickness".[3] Steinleitner aptly characterises the sins that are specified : " Sin and guilt are here related to matters of cult and ritual, not to absolute ethical principles, and so the most important thing is the sinful act itself ; the question of moral responsibility is not raised ".[4] The whole purpose of the atonement procedure is " to make the sinner physically and ceremonially normal again ", being " directed not to his conscience but to his outward appearance ".[5] When a man despises his god, he

[1] It must be remembered that in classical Greek also the gods are concerned with sin : e.g. Plato, Phaedrus 242c ; Laws X, 891e ; Aeschylus, Prom. 945 ; Xenophon, Hist. Gr. I, vii, 19 ; later, Musonius, p. 78, 9, 13. Greek humanism is religious. The gods were identified with the immanent laws of nature. They are embodiments of reality. Here we have something different. [2] Cf. Steinleitner, 83 ff.

[3] Ibid. 99. [4] Ibid. 121.

[5] This view of sin is also found in the examples from the mysteries of Samothrace given by J. Leipoldt in Das Gotterlebnis Jesu, 1927, 35, and Der Sieg d. Christentums über d. antiken Religionen, in Ihmels Festschrift, 1928, 81 f. Cf. Plutarch, Ap. Lac. Antalcidas 1 (II, 217cd), Lysandros 10 (II, 229d), where a confession is required. " It was precisely to sinners that Samothrace was open, and doubtless those concerned were forgiven their sins. But it is uncertain how far sin in this case belongs to the cultic sphere, and how far to the

is not revealing an existential characteristic of human nature, he is simply committing one of the offences already mentioned ; no proper consciousness of sin is indicated.

Plutarch's essay on Superstition contains a passage which is appropriate here : " Let me . . . suffer punishment, unholy and accursed as I am, hated by gods and demons " (II, 168c).[1]

ethical ; those acquainted with Greek religion will understand the difficulty of deciding. The position of Christianity is perfectly clear. Jesus and Paul are indifferent to cultic matters." (Leipoldt, Sieg, 81 f. Cf. Steinleitner, 118 f. ; [L. R. Farnell, Kabeiroi, in E.R.E. VII, 628-632]).

[1] Latte, 294.

VI. SIN IN THE NEW TESTAMENT

I. SYNOPTIC GOSPELS AND ACTS

IT is remarkable how small a part is played by ideas about sin in the Synoptic Gospels, as compared with the rest of the N.T. What they have to say is concerned with two main points : (*a*) Jesus did not talk about the nature and consequences of sin, but he recognised its reality, e.g. in the Sermon on the Mount, and acted accordingly ; (*b*) in word and deed he knew himself to be victorious over sin. These assertions may now be illustrated.

(*a*) The mission of Jesus is to proclaim the Rule of God, which is realised in his words and actions. The historic event brought to pass under this Rule is the conquest of sin. Jesus preaches God as Father, and shows by his works that God is loving, with the result that men recognise that they are far from God in their uncleanness, and long to get back to him. This historic event, brought to pass through the coming of Jesus, is described in the parable of the Prodigal Son, who goes to his father with the confession, "Father, I have sinned against heaven and in thy sight" (Luke xv, 18, 21). Here we see how Jesus understood sin : it is leaving the Father's house, losing touch with him, living without him in the world, with all its pleasure and its sordidness. The historic event, brought to pass by the coming of Jesus, is this recognition of sin and return to God. Jesus here shows, not only what sin is, but also what repentance is, viz. the way to God as the Father who welcomes the sinner with love. "I say to you that even so there

64

shall be joy in heaven over one sinner repenting more
than over ninety-nine good people who have no need
of repentance " (Luke xv, 7, cf. ver. 10). Having
this twofold knowledge, Jesus does not talk about
sin, but preaches of God as the Father, and how he
rules, confident that this will reach the sin, which is
both ungodliness and unneighbourliness,[1] and will
bring about repentance. What gives sin its tragic
importance is that it is guilt towards God.[2]

The truth comes to light in what Jesus does. " I
came not to call the righteous but sinners " (Matt.
ix, 13).[3] This mission explains his behaviour, as
described in the Gospels : " And it came to pass, as
he reclined at meat in the house, behold, many publicans and sinners came and reclined beside Jesus
and his disciples " (Matt. ix, 10 ; cf. ver. 11 and
par. ; Luke xv, 1 f. ; xix, 7). This sort of thing
led to his being called " friend of publicans and
sinners " (Matt. xi, 19 ; Luke vii, 34).[4] The oriental
regards eating together as the expression of the closest
possible fellowship, and in behaving as he does,
Jesus is the conqueror of sin, not only because he puts
an end to the separation of the righteous from sinners,
but also because, by forgiving the sinners, he ends
their separation from God, and by drawing them into
fellowship with himself, creates a new fellowship with

[1] Cf. Matt. xviii, 23 ff. ; v, 21 ff. ; vi, 14 f.

[2] See Matt. vi, 12 ; xviii, 24.

[3] From the fact that Jesus distinguishes between the righteous
and sinners, and yet puts beside the prodigal son the one who
stayed at home but grumbled at his brother's return—a thing
he had seen happening—it is certain that he regarded sin as
universal, and found it in the righteous when confronted by
himself. This explains sayings like Mark viii, 38 ; Luke vi,
32 ff. ; xiii, 1-4. Cf. R.G.G.[2], V, 885, 3.

[4] On the formula, " publicans and sinners ", see J. Jeremias
in Z.N.W., 1931, 293 ff.

God.[1] That is the effect of his pronouncement of forgiveness, which shows him to be the Christ, standing at God's side and endued with power (cf. Matt. ix, 2 ; Luke vii, 47 ff.). Many stories make it clear that by his own behaviour Jesus actually produced the crisis described in the parable of the Prodigal Son : e.g. Luke v, 8 (Peter) ; Luke vii, 37 ff. (the sinful woman) ; Luke xix, 1 ff. (Zacchaeus). His commendation of the publican who prayed, " Have mercy on me, a sinner ", makes it clear that fellowship with himself is God's answer to repentance (Luke xviii, 13 ff.). This admission into fellowship is specially clear in the case of the Prodigal Son. He wants to become one of his father's hired servants. But the father comes to meet him, interrupts his confession, sends for clothing and shoes, and for the ring which is the badge of sonship, crowning his welcome with the sharing of food. The meaning is plain. Man, created for fellowship with God, has broken the fellowship. That is his sin. The arrival of the Kingdom of God restores the fellowship with God, in which Jesus lives, inviting men to share in it by following him.

The same parable makes another point. Those who are righteous object to the behaviour of Jesus towards sinners. The elder son stands for the earnest but joyless worship of the formally righteous (Luke xv, 29), who fail to realise the full meaning of fellowship with God (ver. 31). He is a warning to the Pharisees of the import of what is happening, viz. that Jesus is finding the lost, bringing the dead to life. But the righteous are deaf to his call, and the end of the story is the Cross, which confirms and seals the authority of his words and deeds.

The forgiveness proclaimed and practised by Jesus is something new and extraordinary : it is the defeat

[1] Cf. esp. Schlatter, Matt. 304.

of sin, the breaking in of the Kingdom of God, an eschatological event. He always speaks and acts with authority : that is the great thing. The description of sin and repentance, of the rupture and restoration of fellowship, e.g. in the parable of the Prodigal Son, would make a fine story, wonderfully conceived, but it would never be the life-giving word of forgiveness, unless it came with the authority of Jesus, which is the authority of the eschatological ambassador from God. This connexion becomes perfectly clear at the Last Supper.

The Last Supper is to be associated, on the one hand, with earlier meals, shared by Jesus and his disciples, in which he bound them together as the fellowship of the Kingdom of God (Mark i, 32, the first example ; [1] ii, 15, Capernaum ; vi, 34 ff., Galilee). He often referred to the Kingdom, both directly and indirectly, as a common meal in the Father's House. On the other hand, the Last Supper is to be distinguished from those that went before it, both because it is the last, and because the parabolic action of Jesus gives it a special meaning. The bread he says, means himself as the bread of life ; [2] and the wine means his blood, which seals the founding and inauguration of the institution which embodies the

[1] Ministry (Mark i, 31) means waiting at table.

[2] The expression, " my body, thy body ", etc., often stands in Aramaic for the reflexive pronoun (cf., e.g. John vii, 38 : ἐκ τῆς κοιλίας αὐτοῦ : " from him "). Therefore it may well be possible that for " this is my body " we should read " This am I ". This is supported by our oldest commentary on the words spoken at the Last Supper, viz., John vi (cf. 35, 48, etc.). The first utterance would then indicate the significance of the coming of Jesus : he appears as the bread of life. But his death means the establishment, sealed with blood, of that which is the actual content of his coming, viz. the gift of the Kingdom of God, for the " many ", i.e. for all nations. This is also confirmed by John (cf. xi, 52 ; xii, 32).

Kingdom of God. His mention of the Covenant probably refers to Jer. xxxi, 31-34 : that eschatological promise is now to be fulfilled. The New Covenant is ratified through his coming ; it becomes operative through his death, and will be brought to perfection at the feast in his Father's house, to which he looks forward in his parting words (Mark xiv, 25). Matthew says that his blood, as blood of the Covenant, is "shed for many unto remission of sins ".

The word of forgiveness and the behaviour of Jesus are not simply a matter of course, but something extraordinary ; in them sin is overcome, the Rule of God breaks in ; it is an eschatological event. This is specially clear in the case of the Last Supper, which explains and fulfils the promise of the New Covenant (Jer. xxxi, 31-34) : it is established by the coming of Jesus, and ratified by his death. His blood is covenant blood, "shed for many, for the remission of sins " (Matt. xxvi, 28).[1] This is the fulfilment of Jer. xxxi, 34, and also of Is. liii, 12.[2] Jesus is the Servant of the Lord who takes away the sin of mankind by his suffering and death. This is how he understood his mission. Through his coming, through his death and resurrection, sin is conquered and the foundation is laid for God's new world.

The pronouncement about the unpardonable sin— whether it be a saying of Jesus himself, or a piece of early Christian doctrine, or a genuine saying embroidered by the community—is to be interpreted from this point of view (Matt. xii, 31 f. ; Mark iii, 29) : it means resisting and denouncing the work of Jesus in spite of the conviction that it is the work of the Holy

---

[1] Matt.'s " for the remission, etc." is thoroughly sound interpretation.

[2] Cf. Is. liii, 5 f. The " many " of Matt. and Mark points to Is. liii, 12.

Spirit. The gravity of the situation is revealed : it is the last time ; the Rule of God is breaking in.

To understand fully what sin meant to Jesus, we must observe another point. The Lord's Prayer says, " Forgive us our debts, as we also have forgiven our debtors " (Matt. vi, 12). This noteworthy expression points to man as being in debt. The conception is further illustrated in a number of parables, in which the relation of God to man is likened to those of land-owner to steward, creditor to debtor, employer to employee. The fundamental situation in all these is that, along with life, God has entrusted to man something which belongs to him, in order that he may make profitable use of it. Man is a steward who will be called to account : Matt. xxv, 14 ff. ; Luke xvi, 11 ff. There are two possibilities—faithful-ness and unfaithfulness ; and the latter means being in debt, through misuse, selfish appropriation or squandering of the trust. When this happens, the owner becomes the creditor and the steward the debtor : Luke vii, 41 f. ; Matt. xviii, 23 ff. God loses his property through man's misuse of it ; but loves what he has made and given, and tries to get it back. The function of Jesus is to proclaim this divine activity as forgiving love, and to embody it. Encountering God in this way, and awakening to love and trust, man comes to know God as Father and himself as God's child. Man's breach of crea-turely fellowship with God takes the form of misuse of the gift entrusted to him, and puts him in debt to God. The restoration of fellowship is not only a return, but a new stage of existence : instead of the creaturely relationship, denoted by the symbols, owner-steward and creditor-debtor, there is the real-ised eschatology of Father-son. This is the stage of the forgiveness of debts ; which only operates, however,

when restoration to fellowship with God leads to
the renewal of happy relationships among men with
regard to their debts to one another (Matt. vi, 14 f. ;
xviii, 21 ff.). The Kingdom of God is thus presented
in its totality : if the debtor will neither accept
forgiveness nor grant it to his fellow, God becomes
the Judge. The message and mission of Jesus thus
include the whole complex of sin, debt and forgiveness.

(*b*) Jesus victor over sin—that is the Synoptic
kerygma, based on the facts : " Thou shalt call his
name Jesus, for it is he that shall save his people
from their sins " ('Matt. i, 21).

John the Baptist, as the forerunner of Jesus, makes
sin the focus of all his activity (Matt. iii, 6 ; Mark
i, 4 ; Luke iii, 3). His task as described in the Bene-
dictus (Luke i, 77), is " to give knowledge of salvation
unto his people in the remission of their sins ". He
concentrates on sin, repentance and forgiveness,
because the Kingdom of God is coming. He must
prepare God's people for the New Age, by means of
baptism, which has its prototype in the Flood (I Pet.
iii, 20 f.), and is to be understood as voluntary sub-
mission to the Judgment and deliverance from it.
His mind is filled with the idea that the Judgment is
close at hand. But when Jesus is baptised, the dove
is the sign that God has concluded peace. The
emphasis of Jesus is different, as we have seen, because
he is the fulfiller, who conquers sin, forgiving it in
every word and deed, and brings in the Kingdom of
God.

The story of Jesus is continued in the work of the
apostles, who preach Christ as the saving gift of God,
calling for repentance and baptism in the name of
Jesus Christ for the remission of sins,[1] in clear accord

---

[1] See also Luke xxiv, 47 ; Acts iii, 19 ; xiii, 38 ; xxii, 16 ;
xxvi, 18.

with what he himself did (Acts ii, 38). What differentiates them from him is that they call for the accept-
ance of forgiveness, whereas he actually gives it by
taking sinners into fellowship with himself. They are
" apostles " ; he is the " Lord ". Their preaching
differs from that of the Baptist precisely because they
came after the event, and he before it (see Acts v, 31 ;
x, 43).

It has already been pointed out that in the Synoptic
Gospels and Acts ἁμαρτία always means a particular
act of sin (p. 49). That is why it is almost always
found in the plural. Jesus and the early Church
were not concerned with sin as an intellectual problem ;
they saw it as a reality in men's lives. Christ's business was with this reality. Paul sees sin as an active
force conditioning the world, and deals with it as a
theological problem (see pp. 49, 75 ff.). John stands
nearer to the Synoptists than to Paul.

2. JOHN

Christ's victory over sin, as presented in the earlier
Gospels, meets us again in John's *kerygma*, with the
unfolding of its meaning.[1] The keynote is struck in
I John iii, 5 : " He was manifested to take away sins,
and in him is no sin ". The Christ takes sin upon
himself and removes it. The primary reference is to
his death, and the defeat of sin is pictured in terms
drawn from the Jewish sacrificial system. This is
implied in the quotation above, and appears again at
John i, 29 ; [2] I John ii, 2 ; iv, 10 ; i, 7. Christ

[1] Cf. R. Seeberg, Die Sünden u.d. Sündenvergebung, n.d.
I Joh., in Ihmels Festschrift, 1928, 19 ff.

[2] But cf. C. F. Burney, The Aramaic Origin of the 4th Gospel,
1922, 107 f., where it is suggested that " lamb " is a mistransla-
tion of the Aramaic for " servant ".

defeats the sin of the world as the expiator who makes atonement. This work of his recognises no human limitations of nation, race or sex (I John ii, 2) ; its universal scope is the outcome of his sinlessness (iii, 5). He is the man after God's will, who is one with the Father, and therefore the Son of God. (See John viii, 46 and ix, 16.) [1]

Both aspects of Christ's mission, viz. victory over sin through atonement and the universal significance of this, correspond to the Johannine conception of sin, as defined at I John iii, 4 and v, 17. Sin is behaviour which runs counter to the divine ordinance, which corresponds to what is right ; and so is both ἀνομία and ἀδικία, the contradiction both of what is right and of the will of God. It is in fact the product of the contradiction of God, the outcome of man's godlessness, materialised in unfriendly action. This establishes its universality. Man is not neutral ; he is guilty, and his sin separates him from God (see John ix, 31). This separation is absolute : " He that doeth sin is of the devil, for the devil sinneth from the beginning " (I John iii, 8). The contradiction of God reveals the demonic character of sin, which puts man under the devil's power. " Verily, verily, I say unto you, Every one that committeth sin is the slave of sin " (John viii, 34) : that is no platitude—" verily, verily " shows that—but the truth about man which comes to light through Christ ; human sin is enslave-

[1] The agreement of John with the Synoptists is as clear as the difference between them. They are agreed as to the kerygma. Jesus, as the Christ, is the conqueror of sin. But whereas the first three Gospels give a vivid picture of his outward life among the Jews, John shapes the kerygmatic thesis of the atonement for the sin of the world through the death of the Christ, and thus gives prominence to the guiding principle which found expression at the Last Supper.

ment under demonic power,[1] and so means absolute separation from God.

Christ's coming creates an entirely new situation, best indicated by the word, " crisis ", which means division and decision. He shows up sin as hatred of God (John xv, 22-24), forcing decision upon men and dividing among them (ix, 41). If a man rejects Christ, refusing to believe his " I am " (viii, 24), he remains in his sin and dies in his sin, missing all that Christ came to bring. All other sin is blindness, " unrighteousness, . . . sin not unto death " ; but this, which Christ brings to light, is " sin unto death " (I John v, 16 f.).[2] This is the crisis which came into the world with Christ. The last hour could not be more clearly proclaimed—the hour of decision for life or death. The Jews who turn away from Jesus in hatred face the one possibility, those who believe him the other (I John i, 9). He who acknowledges his guilt before God receives the word of forgiveness. The other cannot receive it because there is no truth in him and he makes God a liar—the diabolic character of sin appearing again (I John i, 8, 10 ; cf. John viii, 44).[3] This situation is not a thing of the past : it is " even now " ; for in the Paraclete Christ abides with his people. The Paraclete continues the work of Christ (John xvi, 8 f.).

Christ's mission, to take away sins, achieves its purpose in the community that is delivered from sin. The affirmation of this deliverance is fundamental, the ground of it being the birth that is of God. Members

[1] It should be noted that Jesus demolishes the claim of the Jews to be the seed of Abraham, and demonstrates their connexion with demons.

[2] Against Seeberg (p. 71, n. 1), 23 ff. [See C. H. Dodd *ad loc.*]

[3] Cf. Hempel (p. 28 n.), 183, in connexion with John viii, 44 : " That is how revelation works : it brings the real situation to light, and so begins the destruction of Satan's kingdom ".

of the community are born again of God through his
free gift of faith, by which they know God and his
Christ. Regeneration is the result of seeing Christ :
" Whosoever abideth in him sinneth not : whosoever
sinneth hath not seen him, neither knoweth him.
Whosoever is begotten of God doeth no sin, because
his seed abideth in him : and he cannot sin, because
he is begotten of God " (I John iii, 6, 9).[1] The new
situation becomes concrete in the community through
the practice of love, which is the exact opposite of
sin. These fundamental assertions are maintained
throughout the Johannine literature, their practical
importance being illustrated in the work of Jesus
(John v, 14) ;[2] but a serious problem is presented by
the fact that they are not substantiated in historical
reality, the Christian community not being sinless.
The new energy of love encounters opposition in its
fight against sin. John is not concerned with the
abstract problem, but deals practically with the
matter in two ways, which serve to emphasise the
fundamental importance of the idea of the sinlessness
of the community. (a) Christ's atonement avails
also for the sin of the community, and the Paraclete
makes it possible to live in a state of tension (I John
ii, 1 f.). (b) The community has the privilege of
prevailing intercessory prayer (I John v, 16).

The Apocalypse describes Christ's work as a work
of love, whereby Christians are delivered out of the
sinful complex of this world : they are set free by his
atoning blood (Rev. i, 5). The task of God's people
in the last days is to avoid all contact with the growing
power of sin, for God's judgment is coming upon the
world to destroy sin and sinners (Rev. xviii, 4 f.).
John sees in his vision a final act of God, putting an

---

[1] Cf. W. Grundmann, Begriff d. Kraft in d. N.T. Gedanken-
welt, 1932, 113, n. 8.   [2] On John v, 14, see p. 75, n. 1.

end to the universal power of sin from which Christians
are set free.[1]

3. PAUL

What Paul says about sin is orientated to the
revelation of God in Christ ; it is not a natural,
empirical doctrine, drawn from a special form of
pessimism, but a divine judgment on godless man,
resulting from that revelation, and seen as stern reality
in the Cross. This is the clue to his teaching on sin,
which may be summarised in two sentences : (a) the
fact of Christ is relevant to man in a particular situation, viz. to man as sinner ; (b) the fact of Christ
comes home to man as release and renewal. What
was fact in the case of Jesus is here described and
unfolded.[2] In this lies the difference between Jesus
and Paul in relation to sin.

(a) Paul owes his conception of sin to the impression
made on him by his own experience of the revelation
of God in Christ. He had regarded himself as blameless according to the ideal of the Law (Phil. iii, 6 ;
cf. Gal. i,14, and see p. 42). That was his self-
consciousness as a Jew. The Damascus experience
led him to confess that he was the least of the apostles,
not worthy to be called an apostle, because he had
persecuted the Church of God (I Cor. xv, 9 ; cf.
I Tim. i, 15). This is his sin (cf. Gal. i, 23 ; Phil.
iii, 6)—the final result of his zeal for the Law, his

[1] The worse thing which may befall the healed man is to die
as the result of committing the " sin unto death " (cf. Schlatter,
Joh. 145). This preserves the link between sin, suffering and
death. But an end is made of the hard and fast logic which
looks for a sinful cause for every case of suffering (John ix, 2 f.),
since it shuts out the working of God in his grace.

[2] Cf. G. Kittel, Die Rel.-gesch. u.d. Urchristentum, 1932,
154 ff., n. 350, for a working out of the general point of view,
which is here applied in detail.

endeavour to attain to salvation along the path of
self-righteousness by works of the Law.   The judgment
upon persecution of the Church of God was also judgment upon that zeal for the Law.   When that dawned
upon him, he realised that all his Jewish practices
were a striving against God's will and amounted to
active enmity against God.   " Man's determination
to manage by himself " [1] is really striving against
God's will.   From the hour in which that became
clear to him, he remained convinced that sin is not
merely an offence against the divine majesty—the
Jew goes that far—but is active hatred towards God,
hostile opposition to his will, on the part of man in
his determination to live for himself and manage by
himself.   This thought of hatred became the constitutive element in the Pauline conception of sin.
The fact that this enmity against God comes to light
in connexion with the Law, and takes the Law into
its service, puts Paul in a hopeless position.   With its
threat of death for the transgressor, the Law guarantees
the very opposite of salvation.   Something more than
the Law is needed, if the Jew is to be saved, and Paul
knew this.   But man is under the Law as long as he
lives (cf. Rom. vii, 1-4), and so the question arises,
how to escape from it.   The answer is, by death
alone!   But that rules out the possibility of salvation.
This situation is fundamentally transformed by the
fact of Christ.   Through his death he is the end of
the Law.   Dying with Christ, man dies to the Law,
to receive salvation in a new life with Christ by means
of faith.   Surrender to Christ in baptism is the real
death of the human ego, which is launched upon a

[1] R. Bultmann, Römer vii u.d. Anthropologie d. Paulus, in
Imago Dei, Festschrift f. G. Krüger, 1932, 53 ff. ; 60 f. : " Sin
is man's determination to be master of his fate, to assert himself,
to be like God ".

new life in the obedience of faith, no longer pleasing itself and managing by itself, but belonging to Christ and under his direction. Dying and rising again with Christ, this ego is dead to enmity with God, and has received reconciliation with God by faith ; it is a new creature. Justification by faith alone is for Paul inseparable from mystical union with Christ.[1]

How does Paul regard sin in the concrete ? This question brings us to Rom. v-viii, of all passages in the N.T. the richest in terms referring to sin. First the fact of Christ is presented : " God commendeth his own love toward us, in that, while we were yet sinners, Christ died for us " (v, 8). Then the meaning of this is explained, in connexion with what has gone before : [2] " . . . as through one man sin entered into the world, and death through sin ; and so death passed unto all men, for that all sinned " (v, 12). Paul gives the Jewish answer to the question concerning the origin of sin : it came into the world through Adam, who freely chose to act against God. And death came too, as wages paid to the hirelings of sin (vi, 23). Thus death's dominion over the world is derived from sin (cf. I Cor. xv, 56). The world is essentially not only something that is created (Rom. i, 20), but also something with sin in it. Although Paul can speak of doom, like Greek and Hellenistic writers—death and doom stand close to each other [3]

[1] Cf. W. Grundmann, Gesetz, Rechtfertigung und Mystik bei Paulus ; Zum Problem der Einheitlichkeit der paulinischen Verkündigung, in Z.N.W., 32 (1933), 52-65.

[2] Rom. v bases the demand for patience in tribulation, by an *a fortiori* argument, on (1) the Christian experience of salvation (v, 7-11), and (2) the new world-situation (v, 12-21).

[3] It must, of course, be remembered that there is a fundamental difference of feeling about life between Greek and Hellenistic dualism and Christianity : " For the former ", as Rohde puts it (see p. 55), " life is the wages of sin ; for the latter, with its consciousness of sin, the wages of sin is death."

—he differs from them in making sin the secret of
death's power. It is the author of all evil. Sin
" reigned the reign of death " (Rom. v, 21 [Moffatt]) :
that is the Christian view, not the Greek. The third
assertion follows from this, viz. that sin, as hostility
towards God, is universal (Rom. iii, 9, 23 ; v, 9 f. ;
viii, 7 ; Gal. iii, 22). Here Paul departs from Judaism,
with its doctrine of individual freedom of choice ;
" through the one man's disobedience the many were
made sinners " : every man shares the common lot
(v, 19). Adam's fall, human mortality, and the
universal propensity to sin are inseparably bound
together. No doctrine of original sin is developed,
but a judgment is expressed upon man as man—
based, it is true, upon the facts of life, but only possible
after the coming of Christ.

What exactly is this propensity to sin ? " For
until the Law ", continues Paul, " sin was in the
world : but sin is not imputed when there is no
Law " (Rom. v, 13). This sentence, linking together the idea of sin and Law, is typically Jewish.
The propensity to sin, already present " in the world"
(cf. vii, 8), is actualised as transgression through the
commandment of the Law (cf. Gal. iii, 19). The
true nature of sin is thus made clear : it is man's self-
assertion in rebellion against God (cf. the basic sin
of Rom. i, 21). This is where sin in general corresponds to the sin of Adam. But it can only be recognised as such after God's will has been declared in
the commandment. Therefore sin between Adam
and Moses is not sin after the likeness of Adam's
transgression (v, 14) ; it is not imputed (13). So
the function of the Law is to actualise the sinful
propensity as transgression, and unveil the true
character of sin as enmity against God (viii, 7) ; to
use an illustration, it is to transform the potential

energy of a state into the kinetic energy of a sinful
act ; and further, to establish guilt and ratify the
death penalty. Sin for Paul is guilt before God, and
as such is man's outstanding characteristic. He thus
absorbs the Jewish conception, deepening and re-
orientating it. He agrees with Judaism in the importance which he attaches to the sinful act when he
establishes the relation between sin and Law ; but the
function of the Law is for him exactly the opposite
of what it is in Judaism.

Paul deals fully with the relation between sin and
Law in Rom. vii. When he speaks of life in the flesh
as a life of sin (vii. 5), he is not identifying sin with
the flesh, as if bodily existence itself constituted sinfulness ; he simply means that sin is in possession. This
is brought to light by the Law (vii, 7-10), which
awakens the slumbering desire and leads to the com-
mission of the sinful act. Desire ($\epsilon\pi\iota\theta\upsilon\mu\iota a$) is not
to be limited to the sensual or sexual sphere, but must
be understood in a comprehensive sense as the mania
for self-assertion over against the claim of God, which
bursts into flame when challenged by the commandment. Here is the nerve of every kind of sin, from
the primal flouting of God (Rom. i, 21) to the sexual
perversions and anti-social crimes and all that further
sinning which Paul sees as the divine punishment of
sin (Rom. i, 24-31 ; I Thess. ii, 16). It is from this
point of view that every single sin committed in this
world assumes importance before God, and the sinner
is found guilty.[1]

[1] The function of the Law is to release desire and disclose its
inmost nature (Rom. vii, 7 ; iii, 20). We are not concerned
here with the functions ascribed to the Law in the dogmatic
teaching about its fourfold meaning [Haggadhah, legal ;
Halakhah, practical ; Peshaṭ, literal ; Ṣodh, mystical], but
with its cosmic and historical function.

It is remarkable that sin should appear here personified as a demon (see pp. 50 ff.). It is indeed demonic in character, as may be seen in the way in which it makes use of God's holy will for its own advancement (Rom. vii, 13) ; the function of the Law in the divine purpose for the world, of which we have already spoken, reaches its culminating point when it shows up sin in its demonic nature as absolute hostility to God. The same characteristic marks the universal propensity to sin since the time of Adam, directed as it is against God. That is why Paul's account of the human situation is completely adequate, when he says, " I am carnal, sold under sin " (Rom. vii, 14). Man is sold as a slave to sin, and consequently under the dominion of death, even before he actually dies (cf. Eph. ii, 1) ; his inner conflict is to be understood in terms of demonic possession (Rom. vii, 15-20) ; and the wages of sin is death (vi, 23).[1] Our examination of Paul's views leads to an important conclusion, viz. that, as in the case of death's dominion, all his references to demons and to Satan are meant to give actuality to his teaching about sin ; they are not the outcome of dualistic speculation, but the testimony of one who sees sin as it really is.

(b) This is the situation which is met by the fact of Christ,[2] who is sent by God to condemn sin and destroy it (Rom. viii, 3). Here is the meaning of the In-

[1] We share Bultmann's interpretation of Rom. vii (R.G.G.[2], IV, 1022) : " Paul is describing the position of the Jew (only the Jew ? W.G.) in its essential meaning, as seen by the believer ". This also appears in his book, Röm. vii u.d. Anthropologie d. Paulus, 53, and is taken up by W. G. Kümmel, Röm. vii. u.d. Bekehrung des P., 1929.

[2] Cf. Hempel, op. cit., 181 : " This recognition of sin in all its terrible power both prepares the way for the gratitude of Rom. vii, 25, and makes the right background for the work of Jesus ".

carnation, so powerfully expressed by Paul in the
arresting words of II Cor. v, 21 : " Him who knew
no sin he made to be sin on our behalf ". The
sinlessness of Jesus is the necessary presupposition of
his being sent. All human sin rests on him, past as
well as present (Rom. iii, 25). Because of Christ
and his defeat of sin, God grants a period of grace,
and judgment is postponed. The fact that God
intends to disclose, judge and destroy the dominion
of sin in Christ enables him to be forbearing before
the plan is carried out, so that both Jews and Gentiles,
whose life and work tend generally in the direction
of God's will, are given a share in salvation, although
they cannot have faith in what God did in Christ.
The recognition of this (Rom. ii, 21-26) rounds off
the preceding argument about judgment according
to works, obedience among the Gentiles and Jewish
disobedience. But now a new way of salvation has
appeared through Christ, in which justification does
not depend on life and work, but solely on faith in
Jesus—and this means a complete re-orientation.
Christ's defeat of sin is described as atonement. Here
lies the importance of his death. It is at the Cross
that sin is defeated once for all (Rom. vi, 10 ; cf.
I Cor. xv, 3 ; Gal. i, 4). That is why the Cross is
the sign of victory over sin, and consequently over
death and demons, and the preaching of the Cross
is the power of God and the wisdom of God (I Cor.
i, 18 ff.). The Cross is inseparable from the Resurrection, without which it would be ineffective (I Cor.
xv, 17). The one historic event, which comprises
them both, is " on our behalf " (II Cor. v, 21 ;
I Cor. xv, 3 ; Gal. i, 4). This is made possible by
the fact that, in Paul's view, men are not isolated
individuals, but are bound together in a common
destiny of sin and death by Adam's sin. The fact of

6

Christ gives men victory over sin and the beginning
of the mastery of life. It is the turning point of time
(Rom. v, 21).

When this comes home to man, it literally saves
him from sin and sets his life upon a new foundation.
Here is the Gospel, viz. that through faith and baptism
a man is justified, becomes a new creature, risen with
Christ, reconciled, redeemed—in a word, that he
obtains the forgiveness of sins (cf. Eph. i, 7).[1]
Christians share in Christ's death by faith, and their
union with him is perfected in baptism (Rom. vi, 2 f.).
The theme of Rom. vi is : the Christian and sin.
Throughout the chapter runs the fundamental conviction that the Christian is set free from sin. He is
dead to sin because he has died with Christ (ver. 6) :
the meaning of the fact of Christ is realised in him ;
he exemplifies the old familiar thesis : " he that hath
died is justified " (ver. 7).[2] Further, he is free from
the Law and its function as the releaser of sin (ver. 14) ;
and finally, he is no longer the slave of sin (18-22).
The Christian must bear all this in mind, and draw
the consequences of the principle laid down in ver. 16.
There can be no question of remaining in sin and
sinning as though nothing had happened—in order
that grace may abound (vv. 1, 15) ! On the con-

[1] Actually Paul only uses ἄφεσις at Eph. i, 7 [and Col. i, 14],
though he has the verb in a quotation at Rom, iv. 7 [and has
χαρίζεσθαι at Eph. iv, 32 and Col. ii, 13 ; iii, 13]. Many other
words come in for consideration here, e.g. βαπτίζω, δικαιόω,
καταλλάσσω, ἀπολύτρωσις, σύν, etc. We can only deal here
with certain ideas relevant to our subject.

[2] K. G. Kuhn, Z.N.W., 1931, 105 ff. : " The recognition that
Paul in Rom. vi, 7 is quoting a piece of Rabbinical theology
makes the argument clear and simple : our old man is crucified
with Christ, and that does away with the body of sin, so that
we are no longer under the necessity of serving sin—in accordance
with the principle that he who dies is acquitted of sin because
of his death ".

trary, dying to sin means living to God (11 f.), a new possibility described by Paul in various ways in vv. 13-19. Sanctification (19, 22) means a life of holiness, devoted to God, and is the object to be achieved by the fact of Christ (cf. ἵνα in Rom. viii, 3 f. and II Cor. v, 21). This is significantly implied in the τύπος τῆς διδαχῆς of ver. 17. Τύπος is the moulding pattern ; διδαχή the teaching which regulates conduct. These terms cannot refer to a thing ; they must mean a person.[1] For one who has died and risen again with Christ, i.e. for his ego, Christ has become the pattern, shaping his conduct. Τύπος τῆς διδαχῆς is Christ. The fellowship with Christ, which begins with the sharing of death and resurrection, and means ultimately the gift of sonship, grows in this way until it is perfected in the sharing of glory (viii, 15-17). It is a life of faith. Freedom from sin finds its fulfilment in the obedience of faith (Rom. xiv, 23), and the new life of faith, which is lived unto God, shows itself in brotherly love, which is the fulfilling of the Law (cf. I Cor. viii, 12).

The Christian is in a state of tension between two actualities. Fundamentally he is delivered from sin, redeemed, reconciled and sinless ; as a matter of fact he is at war with sin, which is still threatening, aggressive and dangerous. So he must be summoned to sanctification.[2] The true state of affairs is described in Rom. viii, 10 : in his bodily life the Christian is given up to death, in which sin finally works itself out ; but he has a new spiritual life from Christ, with whom he has died and risen again, and is under the

---

[1] Not " the Christian doctrine " (Zahn), or " the Pauline mode of teaching " (Kühl), or " Christianity " (Lietzmann). Schlatter takes a step in the right direction (Gerechtigkeit Gottes ad loc.), but does not proceed to the proper conclusion.

[2] See Grundmann, Begriff d. Kraft, etc., 79 f., 108 ff.

possession of a new Spirit (viii, 11, in contrast to vii, 18, 20). This spiritual life has overcome death, and springs from the mastery of life which began with Christ, and is to be perfected in the complete destruction of sin and death at his second coming (Rom. viii, 11 ; I Cor. xv, 26). The ego, the inward man, has already died and been delivered from death through fellowship with Christ ; he is with Christ, though the body be dead (Phil. i, 23), and at the resurrection of the dead this ego receives a new body of glory, no longer hidden but manifested with Christ. The present state of tension belongs to the time of waiting " for the glory which shall be revealed to us-ward " (Rom. viii, 18).

4. HEBREWS, JAMES, I PETER

(a) The Epistle to the Hebrews deals with sin from the point of view of the part played by the high priest and sacrifice under the old covenant in the ritual of atonement (Heb. v, 1). Christ is preached as the eternal high priest who has wrought atonement and taken away sins by the offering of himself as a sacrifice. His sinlessness differentiates him from the human high priest (iv, 15 ; v, 3 ; vii, 26 f.), and his one historic self-sacrifice has achieved that removal of sin which is beyond the power of the whole sacrificial system (x, 2-4, 11 ; ix, 26). Thus an end is put to that system, for the fact of Christ has brought salvation in the remission of sins (x, 18). This inaugurates the Messianic age, which is moving towards its climax (ix, 26-28)—the age of forgiveness foretold by the prophets (viii, 12 ; x, 17 ; cf. i, 3 ; ii, 17 ; x, 12).

The Christian community is exhorted to meet persecution by laying aside the sin that clings so closely, resisting unto blood, i.e. martyrdom, in the fight against it (xii, 1-4 ; cf. iii, 13). The warning is emphasised by a reference to the unpardonable sin (x, 26), which involved the whole problem of the struggles over repentance in the early Church. Conscious falling away from faith is unforgivable, though it differs from the sin against the Holy Spirit in the Synoptic Gospels and its Johannine "crisis" formulation. Early Christianity here shows its martyr spirit.

(b) The Epistle of James moves on Jewish lines. The root of sin in man is desire (ἐπιθυμία), which corresponds exactly to the [Rabbinical] evil inclination. The illustration of conception and birth is used to show what happens. A man is tempted by desire, and when he consents, desire conceives and brings forth a sin. But that is not the end of the process, for when the sin is full-grown, it brings forth death (James i, 15). Desire, sin and death are connected with one another by a necessary natural process. The reference is to a definite act of sin, as at ii, 9 and iv, 17—the latter a sin of omission. The end of the Epistle deals with matters connected with repentance : intercession procures God's forgiveness of sins ; confession before a brother is recommended, and in cases of sickness is regarded as a condition of healing ; it is the duty of a Christian to guard his brother against sin, or to save him from it, this availing for atonement (v, 15-20). The aim of the Epistle throughout is practical.

(c) I Peter sets forth the sinless Christ as victorious over sin in terms of the Servant of the Lord of Isaiah xl ff. (I Pet. ii, 22, 24 ; iii, 18). It is further stated that separation from sin shows itself in willing suffering for Christ's sake (iv, 1), because here self-interest submits to the will of God. Finally, genuine love to one another is enjoined, on the ground that " love

covereth a multitude of sins " (iv, 8). Sin is overcome by forgiveness in Jesus Christ and the life of
love. The thought of love as covering sins and saving
is also found at James v, 19 f., and I John iii, 17 f.,
v, 16 ff. point in the same direction. This early
Christian teaching goes back to the teaching of Jesus.
The forgiveness brought by Jesus and the love that
forgives a brother and takes care of him—these fill
out the Christian life and bring the dominion of sin
to an end.

VII. CONCLUSION

WHEN we review the course of our argument, one thing stands out as the heart of the Gospel : Christ has removed the last obstacle to salvation by his victory over sin. This creates a new world-situation. The distinguishing feature of the message of the New Testament, that which gives it its decisive quality, is its eschatological sense of history, its conviction that the final stage of the fulfilment of God's purpose for this world has been inaugurated : a new world is breaking in because Christ has conquered sin.[1] The important point is the stress on his victory, and there is good reason for this in the fact that the special character of Christianity is to be found in its attitude to sin. This has been pointed out, on the historical side, by R. Reitzenstein and K. Latte, and on the theological side by K. Holl and G. Kittel, and we shall quote their words.

R. Reitzenstein, Poimandres 180 A 1 : " What is new seems to me to be that this redemption is not merely getting rid of evil passions and burdens, escaping from death and securing eternal life, but

[1] This point of view has been brought to the fore by Bultmann's criticism of Holl in Theol. Rundsch., 1932, 1 ff., and is proving fruitful in the discussion of the relation of early Christianity to the history of religion. But cf. also Kittel, Probleme, 130 f. ; Rel. gesch. u. Urchr. 151 f., n. 315, where Bultmann's generalisation is applied to Jesus and the Synoptists. There is really no need to follow Bultmann in his radical disagreement with Holl, since the eschatological point of view necessarily involves the proclamation of a conviction about God, man and the world, that is quite unique, and justifies its sense of history by an appeal to truth.

above all the forgiveness of sins. Hellenism, so far as I can see, lacks the tremendous earnestness of the preaching of guilt and atonement. . . . When the early Christians brought together the death of Jesus and this deep feeling of guilt and belief in the forgiveness of the worst guilt, then, for the first time, the Christian Saviour-doctrine found its unique, world-conquering strength ; its Hellenistic rivals could do no more than prepare the way for it in a world that had recovered the consciousness of sin."

K. Latte, Schuld und Sünde in der griechischen Religion, 298 : " When Paul separates sin from all other forms of evil, taking an exclusively moral view of it, and gives prominence to the gracious act of God, whereby man's sin and weakness are covered, redemption comes to mean primarily the forgiveness of sins. . . . In spite of all its efforts, the heathen world had failed to reach a clear formulation of this idea. The new religion owed to Paul a very real part of its growing strength." By way of criticism it should be pointed out that " an exclusively moral view " is not true to the N.T., which takes a theological view, and is only moral in so far as the claim of God covers social behaviour. The rest of the terminology may be accepted with the same proviso.

K. Holl, Urchristentum und Religionsgeschichte, Zeitschr. Syst. Theol., 1924, 399 ff., esp. 425 : " A mystery which offered the remission of sins would have been a monstrosity to the Greeks." [See p. 89.]

G. Kittel, Die Lebenskräfte der ersten christlichen Gemeinden (1926), 19 ff. : " An entirely different problem dominates Christian thinking. Christianity is the sinner's religion. The sinner stands before God." (See also Kittel's Urchristentum, Spätjudentum, Hellenismus, 1926, 27, and his reply, in Th. Lit. Bl., 1929, 373 f., to the objections of J. Leipoldt in

Das Gotteserlebnis Jesu, 1927, 35. (See p. 62 n. 5 for Leipoldt's later agreement ; as a historian of ideas he has no use for eschatology, and so does not get beyond relativity.) Kittel has further developed his theme in Die Religionsgeschichte und das Urchristentum, 1932, 118 ff. : " This religion, while never for a single moment ceasing to be a moral religion, calls a halt at the fact of non-fulfilment (of God's commandment). This is the religion, at the centre of which stands the consciousness of having failed to do what ought to have been done, the consciousness of sin (120). . . . " The first place is given to victory over guilt, over sin, and after that, over death, the wages of sin (122). . . . The announcement of forgiveness is always for the early Church the announcement of Christ. In Christ the holiness of God is the judging of sin ; and in Christ the love of God is the saving of the sinner (124)."

This is the view which our argument has established. It may be stated finally in three propositions : (i) sin is as fundamental a characteristic of this world as the fact that it has been created ; (ii) sin is man's rebellious self-assertion over against the claim of God, not only on the part of certain Promethean individuals, but universally, as an essential of all human existence ; and (iii) the whole meaning of redemption is concentrated in the forgiveness of sins. This is what distinguishes Christianity from Hellenism and from Judaism. To understand this is to understand the fact of Christ.

[*Note.* There is a good presentation of Holl's views in O. S. Rankin, Israel's Wisdom Literature (1936), 40-44.]

INDEX

(Scripture references are to the English Bible; where Hebrew and/or Greek enumeration differs, this is shown throughout the book.)